Famous Animals of the States

Famous Animals of the States

TRUE-TO-LIFE TALES OF THE
MOST UNUSUAL BEASTS OF THE
50 STATES, PUERTO RICO, AND THE
DISTRICT OF COLUMBIA

by Paul D. Buchanan

McFarland & Company, Inc., Publishers
Jefferson, North Carolina, and London

Front cover photo: Mildred the Bear (North Carolina). Photo courtesy Hugh Morton (Grandfather Mountain)

British Library Cataloguing-in-Publication data are available

Library of Congress Cataloguing-in-Publication Data

Buchanan, Paul D., 1958–
    Famous animals of the states : true-to-life tales of the most unusual beasts of the 50 states, Puerto Rico, and the District of Columbia / by Paul D. Buchanan.
      p. cm
    Includes bibliographical references and index.
    ISBN 0-7864-0146-X (sewn softcover : 55# alk. paper) ∞
    1. Famous animals — United States.   I. Title.
QL793.B83   1996
591.973 — dc20

                             96-18685
                               CIP

Manufactured in the United States of America

McFarland & Company, Inc., Publishers
  Box 611, Jefferson, North Carolina, 28640

To
Penni, Jason, and Lily

ACKNOWLEDGMENTS

MY THANKS TO:

The American Morgan Horse Association
Cathy Bagaglio, Como Zoo, St. Paul, Minnesota
LeRoy Barnett, Michigan State Department
Ruth Bartels, State Historical Society of Iowa
Evelyn Bechtel, New Hampshire Historical Society
Susan Biggs, National Zoological Park, Smithsonian Institution
Jennifer Bosley, Colorado Historical Society
Nicollete Bromberg, State Historical Society of Wisconsin
Carla Cisero, Museum of Vertebrate Zoology, Berkeley
Julie Cline, Washington and Lee University
Bill Deely, Punxsutawney Ground Hog Club
Sandy Destiny, Louisiana State University
Philipp Earl, Nevada Historical Society
John L. Fergusen, Arkansas History Commission
Charles Finsley, Dallas Museum of Natural History
Carol Flammer, Zoo Atlanta
P. Gemey, Astoria Public Library
James Hagler, U.S. Space and Rocket Center
Wendy Haynes, The New York Historical Society
Patricia Henighan, Arizona–Sonora Desert Museum
Nilda M. Jiminez, Caribbean Stranding Network
Margaret Johnson, Nevada State Library and Archives
Joy Jordan, Centennial Memorial Library, Eastland, Texas
Gladi Kulp, State of Alaska Library of Education
John Lee, New York Racing Association
Chuck Lennox, Woodland Park Zoo, Seattle, Washington
Terry Lincoln, Dakota Zoo, Bismarck, North Dakota
Norman McCorkle, South Carolina Department of Archives & History
Elizabeth Chadbourn McKee, University of Arkansas Library, Fayetteville
Susan McNeil-Marshall, Hinsdale Public Library
Catherine Morton, Grandfather Mountain

Julie Mulvihill, University of Kansas Natural History Museum
Eric Mundell, Indiana Historical Society
Donald F. Nell, Lewis & Clark Trail Heritage Foundation, Inc.
Eloise Potter, North Carolina State Museum of Natural History
James E. Potter, Nebraska State Historical Society
Lori Rader, Rapid City Public Library, South Dakota
Patricia Redfearn, The Rhode Island Historical Society
Maile Sakamoto, Hawaii Division of Forestry and Wildlife
Mindy Schemberg, Baltimore Zoo
Janet B. Schwarz, Virginia Historical Society
Marty Shock, University of Arkansas, Fayetteville
Ed Shoemaker, Oklahoma Historical Society
Rebecca A. Smith, Historical Society of Southern Florida
Lynne Swanson, Laramie County Library, Wyoming
Ann Taylor, Arizona Historical Society
Raymond Teichman, Franklin D. Roosevelt Library
Jennifer Tolpa, Massachusetts Historical Society
George L. Voit, South Carolina Historical Society
Sibyelle Zemitis, California State Library

And Penni Thorpe, photographic consultant and partner

TABLE OF CONTENTS

PREFACE

What makes the study of history so fascinating is that it provides limitless material from which to draw. The more specifically one focuses on a certain personality, place, or event, the wider the variety of anecdotes one uncovers. This is true for the largest continent and the smallest nomadic village. And every story — no matter how great or how small — is an intricate piece in the complete puzzle of history. It is from this premise, in part, that *Famous Animals of the States* was born.

The other inspiration for this book is much simpler: an early, almost instinctive love of animals. Even in childhood, I was enthralled by the idea that I shared the planet with other creatures, vastly different from myself, yet motivated by the same basic needs and drives. I incorporated animals into my playtime, imagining myself the wolf, the eagle, the crocodile, the octopus, or the sea lion. Even then, I knew that someday I could learn a great deal from the beasts of the field — certainly much more than they could ever learn from me.

The project that became this book started with a very simple question: *What is the single most famous animal in the history of your state?* Beginning in July 1994, this question was sent to reference librarians from historical societies and public libraries throughout the fifty states, three major territories, and the District of Columbia. Their responses became the source for the stories in *Famous Animals of the States*. Most of the librarians and historians responded right away, either with a nomination of their own, or another source for nominations. Some of those surveyed nominated more than one animal. Some did not respond, in which case other institutions, such as newspapers or state libraries, were contacted. The result is a collection of stories that is all the more fascinating because the tales are absolutely true.

Actually, the survey began as a lark of sorts. I had no real notion of how many would respond to the survey, nor did I even know what kinds of stories I was seeking. I sent the initial surveys out merely to see what would happen. As an avid reader of newspapers, I know that each week there is usually at least one story of some animal doing some amazing thing. Therefore I assumed there was plenty of story material from which to draw. Even so, the number and

1

content of the responses was amazing. My initial assumption was certainly proven correct.

For Hawaii, Delaware, and Arkansas, a species or subspecies was chosen, rather than one individual creature. The reason for this is because (1) no single animal was nominated and (2) the species' story was so unusual and so pertinent to the life and history of the state that its inclusion was deemed appropriate. In all other cases, the stories are about specific, individual, named animals whose lives had some extraordinary impact on the surrounding communities.

Once I received a state's nomination for "most famous animal," it fell upon me to conduct additional research — not only about the specific animal, but also about the species which that animal represented, and the geography and history of the area from which it came. Through the process I learned about the animals, the states, the history of the states — and a great deal about human nature.

As a social worker currently working with elderly and dependent adults, I have long noticed how very important — in some cases, life-sustaining — animals can be to people. I have known individuals who, on the brink of eviction from their homes, preferred to live on the streets rather than move into an apartment building that would not accept their pets. Animals bring wonder, excitement, companionship, and purpose to many, many lives that otherwise would be painful and lonely in the extreme.

There is no doubt that the fates of animals and human beings are intertwined, both in the wilderness and in the neighborhood. What is unusually striking about these stories is how much these particular animals affected the lives and emotions of the people that knew them, or knew of them. These creatures inspire love, hate, awe, terror, envy, grief, celebration, mystery, inspiration, and vilification. Each one is remembered in the lore of its community, and each contributed, in its own way, to the rich history of its state.

There are, no doubt, many famous animals that have been left out, many stories that have not yet been brought to this writer's awareness. This book was not intended to be a comprehensive study, to encompass all the notable animals that ever lived in the United States. Rather, it is a sampling of the kinds of anecdotes which are so wonderfully abundant in history.

AMERICAN ANIMAL CHRONOLOGY

1775   Unnamed horse carries Paul Revere on his ride (MA)
1778   Captain Cook meets the Nene (HA)
1789   Justin Morgan is foaled (VT)
1805   Scannon arrives with Lewis and Clark at Ft. Clatsop (OR)
1822   The Chepachet elephant is shot (RI)
1861   Old Abe becomes mascot of Company C (WI)
1862   Arab marches to Manassas (SC)
1864   Traveller carries General Lee to Appomattox Court House (WV)
1876   Comanche is found alive at Little Bighorn (KS)
1883   Old Mose kills Jake Radcliff (CO)
1885   Jumbo is killed by a freight train (CT)
1887   Punxsutawney Phil prognosticates for the first time (PA)
1888   Old Charlie is buried at sea (NB)
1895   Peter the Great is purchased by J. Malcolm Forbes (MI)
1900   Jim Butler's burro discovers Tonopah Mine (NV)
1901   Steamboat appears in a rodeo for the first time (WY)
1902   The teddy bear is invented (MS)
1906   Dan Patch sets the world record for the mile (IN)
1908   Old Ben travels the carnival circuit (IN)
1910   Martha becomes the last passenger pigeon (OH)
1916   Razorbacks become the Arkansas mascot (AK)
1918   Gen. Pershing raises $7316.50 for the Red Cross (IA)
1919   Man o' War is beaten by Upset (KY)
1920   The Custer wolf is killed (SD)
1923   Old Rip appears at the Eastland Country Courthouse (TX)
1925   Balto leads the heroic sled team into Nome (AK)
1928   Chinook is lost in the Antarctic (NH)
1936   Shep appears at Ft. Benton for the first time (MT)
1937   Big Medicine sires Little Medicine (MT)
1939   The Blue Hen becomes the state bird (DE)

1941 Mary Ann dies at Druid Hill Park Zoo (MD)
1944 Fala has his finest moment (NY)
1945 Blaze bumps three servicemen in Memphis (TN)
1948 Shasta the Liger is born (UT)
1950 Smokey Bear is so named (NM)
1953 Sharlie is given its name (ID)
1955 George L. Mountainlion dies (AZ)
1956 Mike the Tiger dies at LSU (LA)
1959 Miss Baker flies in a Jupiter rocket (AL)
1961 Willie B. the gorilla comes to the Atlanta Zoo (GA)
1963 George joins the army (NC)
1964 Flipper airs on NBC (FL)
1968 Mildred arrives at Grandfather Mountain (NC)
1969 Morris appears in his first commercial (IL)
1970 Secretariat is foaled (VA)
1971 Snoopy comes home (OK)
1972 Koko signs "drink" (CA)
1973 Andre goes to the New England Aquarium (MA)
1977 Bozo stars in "Grizzly Adams" (WA)
1978 Charlie Chan inherits $250,000 (MO)
1985 Humphrey returns to the Pacific Ocean (CA)
1987 Clyde dies (ND)
1989 Sparky Show Amphitheatre is dedicated (MN)
1990 Taro attacks little girl in Trenton (NJ)
1991 Ling Ling dies of old age (DC)

FAMOUS ANIMALS
OF THE STATES

Alabama

ANIMAL: Miss Baker
DOB: June 29, 1957
DOD: November 25, 1984
DESCRIPTION: Squirrel monkey (*Saimiri oerstedii*), 11 ounces, white and
brown fur.

The United States' status in the space race was in tremendous jeopardy
by 1959. Sputnik, the first artificial satellite, was launched by the USSR in 1957.
All American attempts to place a living being — usually a monkey or a mouse —
into space had failed; every animal sent up in a rocket had died as a result of
the stresses of rocket travel. Things were looking grim for the U.S. space program.

Then along came one who would come to be known as the "first lady of
space." She was Miss Baker, an 11-ounce, two-year-old squirrel monkey, a
native of Iquitos, Peru. Normally, a squirrel monkey's life would consist of
scrambling through trees, hunting for fruits and insects and seeds to eat, and
keeping a sharp lookout for predators such as the harpy eagle. However, the
destiny of this particular primate was about to take a spectacular twist. On
May 29, 1959, Miss Baker, in the company of a seven-pound rhesus monkey
from Fort Knox, Kentucky, named Able, blasted off from Cape Canaveral,
Florida, in the nose cone of a Jupiter rocket. The "monkeynauts," as they were
dubbed, wore molded plastic helmets and were strapped onto a fiberglass and
rubber couch in a semi-fetal position, to minimize the effects of the gravita-
tional pressures they were about to endure. During their space flight, Able and
Baker would be studied for the effects of noise, acceleration, deceleration,
vibration, rotation, and the gravity-free state. The monkeynauts were accompanied by samples of mustard seeds, corn, yeast, fruit fly larvae, human blood,
mold spore, and fish eggs — all of which would be examined to determine how
they had been affected by space travel.

During the course of their 1700-mile journey, the monkeynauts attained
an altitude of 350 miles and a speed exceeding 10,000 miles per hour. The
pair endured forces 38 times stronger than the pull of gravity. After ninety
minutes, the nose cone splashed down at Antigua in the Atlantic Ocean. Both
monkeys survived without injuries or apparent complications.

According to monitors activated during the flight, Miss Baker became startled during lift-off and at other times during the flight. Upon meeting with
her handlers immediately after the flight, she gave one of them a sharp bite
on the hand (possibly to thank him for the experience). She was given a banana
and a cracker; then she simply rolled on her side and fell asleep.

Unfortunately, Able was not so lucky. The flight's impact on the rhesus monkey manifested itself a few days later. On an operating table at Fort Knox, Kentucky, Able died due to the effects of the anesthetic used while army doctors attempted to remove an electrode used to monitor her heartbeat during the spaceflight. Before the flight, Able had taken some trichloroethylene without ill effects. But the stress of the flight apparently affected the monkey's metabolism to the point that her body could no longer handle the anesthetic. Able's death was a great tragedy for the space program; the army's space medicine chief said it was something that "makes you want to kick in a door."

But Miss Baker survived, and continued to thrive for years afterward. After her space flight, she was sent to the School of Aviation Medicine in Pensacola, Florida. There she met another squirrel monkey named Big George, who would be her companion for the next 19 years.

In 1971, Miss Baker and Big George moved to the Alabama Space and Rocket Center in Huntsville, where the Jupiter rocket in which Baker had flown 12 years earlier had been built. The couple cohabited in a glass-plated, split-level home. During their years together, Miss Baker and Big George made an appearance on the "Dinah Shore Show," frolicking with guests George Carlin and Sandy Duncan for a national television audience. Walter Cronkite and CBS featured Miss Baker's twentieth birthday in 1977, and national headlines and television coverage captured her twenty-fifth birthday in 1982.

When Big George died in 1979, a male squirrel monkey named Norman moved to Huntsville from the Yerkes Primate Center in Atlanta, Georgia. The "wedding" of Norman and Miss Baker took place on April 9, 1979. It was officiated by Judge Dan McCoy of Huntsville, and more than 500 visitors and local residents attended the ceremony. While in residence at the Space and Rocket Center, Miss Baker received fan mail from children from all over the United States who had studied about her 1959 flight. Thousands of visitors traveled to the Alabama Space and Rocket Center over the years to pay homage to the first lady of space. In 1979, the mayor of Huntsville even proclaimed Miss Baker's birthday, June 29, as "Monkeynaut Baker Day."

Miss Baker, the first passenger to survive an American space flight and the oldest squirrel monkey in captivity, died on November 25, 1984, at the age of 27, as a result of respiratory complications following acute kidney failure. Miss Baker was buried near the entrance to the space museum in a wooded grove. A five-foot stone marks the location.

In the wake of her death, Edward O. Buckbee, then director of the Space and Rocket Center, said, "She will be missed by all of us who knew her and those thousands of visitors who came to know this tiny squirrel monkey. For future visitors to the center, there will be something missing. A part of space flight history won't be there to greet them."

SOURCES: Tremain, Ruthven. *The Animals' Who's Who.* New York: Charles Scribner's Sons. Pg. 1. / U.S. Space and Rocket Center, Huntsville, Alabama. News releases and articles.

Alaska

ANIMAL: Balto
DOB: Between 1920 and 1922
DOD: Probably between 1930 and 1935
DESCRIPTION: Alaskan malamute, 22" tall at shoulder, 52 pounds, dark gray.

The year 1925 was the era of the diphtheria scourge, better known as the Black Death. Diphtheria is a highly contagious disease which produces a poison throughout the body. It creates a thick membrane in the throat which may interfere with eating, drinking, and breathing. The poison is harmful to tissues of the heart, the central nervous system, and the lymph glands. If not treated, diphtheria results in fatalities from heart and kidney failure. In mid–January 1925, two Eskimo children became infected and died, causing health officials to fear that an epidemic of Black Death could wipe out the population around the entire area of Nome.

Enter Balto the Sled Dog. So revered are this Alaskan malamute's efforts in bringing serum to the residents of Nome that a statue in his honor stands in New York City's Central Park — even though Balto's story comes from Nome, Alaska. That year there was a terrible winter in Alaska. The railroad between Anchorage and Nome was buried in snow at Nenana, 674 miles from Nome. All the available planes in those days had open cockpits, and the possibility of the planes operating in sub-zero weather was uncertain. Therefore, it was decided that the serum would be transported by dog sled team — 20 teams of dogs carrying the serum in 20 pounds of specially insulated packaging material.

The final run of the mission began at Bluff, Alaska, on February 1, some 53 miles from Nome. The musher was Gunnar Kassen, a Norwegian with 21 years of sled-driving experience. Five miles down the trail, the dogs were belly-deep in a snowdrift. In the numbing darkness, the team, led by Balto, found its way around the drift, and eventually back on the trail. Soon afterward, the team arrived at the banks of the frozen Topkok River.

Suddenly, Balto stopped, refusing to move any farther. Kassen shouted at the lead dog, imploring him to move. Balto stood his ground. Finally, the frustrated Kassen charged to the front of the team and found Balto standing in shallow water. The ice was cracking, and Balto's instincts for survival had saved the entire team from plunging into the river.

After Kassen had dried Balto's paws, the team continued in the darkness. Balto followed his instincts, moving ever forward. At one frantic point, a sudden gust of wind overturned the sled and several dogs. Momentarily, the serum was lost. Groping for several panic-stricken moments, barehanded and blind

Gunnar Kasson + Balto in their Race to Nome.

BALTO AND GUNNAR KASSON
(courtesy of Siberian Husky Club of America)

in the snow, Kassen finally located the serum package and loaded it back on the sled.

At 2:00 A.M., Kassen, Balto, and the team arrived at Point Safety, some 25 miles from Nome. The team was supposed to be relieved by musher Ed Rohn and another sled. But Kassen, anxious over the lost time of his relay, and confident that his team could continue, mushed the dogs on. Balto led the team until they reached Nome at 5:30 A.M. on February 2, 1925.

The media went wild over Balto and Kassen. A statue commemorating Balto and "The Great Race of Mercy to Nome" was cast in bronze and placed in New York's Central Park.

This celebration of Balto caused some controversy and discontent among the mushers. Leonhard Seppala, a champion dog sled musher and once the owner of Balto, claimed the dog had received unjustified acclaim. He said the real hero of the relay was his favorite racing dog, Togo, who led the eighteenth leg of the journey. While Balto and his team traveled 53 miles from Bluff to Nome, Togo's team — driven by Seppala, who apparently was miffed when the media ignored him — had traveled 91 miles from Shatoolik to Golovin. In addition, complained Seppala, Togo was a champion racer, while Balto was but a lumbering freight dog.

But the Balto backers felt the acclaim was more than justified. Balto's strength and intelligence saved the team and the race from a tragic, frozen end. In addition, they felt that Balto, an ordinary dog, better epitomized the more than 100 dogs that ran in the race and therefore was a more appropriate symbol of the entire incredible adventure. In any case, the story of Balto serves as an emblem of heroism in the worst of times, and bravery at the edge of tragedy.

SOURCES: Ricker, Elizabeth M. *Seppala: Alaskan Dog Driver.* Boston: Little, Brown, 1930. Pp. 294–295. / Sherwonit, Bill. *Iditarod: The Great Race of Nome.* Anchorage: Alaska Northwest, 1960. Pp. 31–40. / Standiford, Natalie. *The Bravest Dog Ever.* New York: Random House, 1989.

Arizona

ANIMAL: George L. Mountainlion
DOB: February 1952
DOD: March 8, 1955
DESCRIPTION: Mountain lion (*Puma concolor*), approximately 5' long, approximately 175 pounds.

On November 5, 1953, a new column appeared in the *Arizona Daily Star.* Although the column itself was an unusual and interesting feature, it was the columnist that attracted the attention of Tucson, Arizona — for the columnist's name was George L. Mountainlion.

Actually, George had come to the Arizona–Sonora Desert Museum in February 1953 from California, where he was to share his enclosure with the then-resident mountain lion, Susie. Unable to get along with George, Susie was soon removed. But George stayed on, fascinating and charming more than 100,000 visitors to the museum each year.

In 1953, William H. Carr, a cofounder of the museum, was writing a column for the *Arizona Daily Star* called "Trailside Topics." One day the managing editor of the *Star*, Jack Weadock, commented on how attractive an animal George was, and how something special should be done in the column to highlight him. It was suggested that the readers might be interested in a column from the mountain lion's point of view. The editor readily agreed, and on November 5, 1953, the column had a new by-line. From that point on, "Trailside Topics by George L. Mountainlion" appeared in the Sunday *Arizona Daily Star*, with several ghostwriters contributing over the years.

The column featured stories about the animals of the Arizona–Sonora Desert Museum. This museum (founded in 1952), located ten miles west of Tucson, was established in 1955 as an independent community educational institution. Its purpose is to provide information on the desert life surrounding the Tucson area. It features displays of large and small species of the Sonora Desert, a desert garden, a walk-in aviary, the Beaver–Otter–Bighorn Sheep Complex, and the Congdon Earth Sciences Center, highlighting underground cave life and geology. And, of course, the main attraction over the years has been its mountain lion.

Actually, mountain lions — *Puma concolor*, also known as pumas, cougars, catamounts, and other monikers — rarely make it as Sunday newspaper columnists. As the only large cat indigenous to the United States, the mountain lion is often regarded as the most magnificent animal in the country. Unfortunately, it has also achieved a reputation as a dangerous animal, although attacks upon humans are extremely rare. Spontaneous attacks occur most often during times of extended drought, when the cat's usual prey — anything from deer to rabbits and raccoons — moves closer to water sources, which are often close to human developments. Normally, mountain lions are shy, secretive animals, which is why human attempts to study the beast have revealed relatively little.

The range of the mountain lion — in Arizona or anywhere in the United States — is often a matter for extensive speculation. The big cat no doubt inhabits expansive territory in Arizona, where much of the land is untouched by humans. But again, because of the species' inconspicuous habits, mapping the habitats of mountain lions can be a frustrating and even futile endeavor.

Over the years — particularly in the late nineteenth to early twentieth century — ranchers saw mountain lions as threats to livestock, and efforts to exterminate them grew to nearly maniacal levels. No doubt cougars have taken their share of domestic cattle and sheep over the decades, particularly during those times of drought when natural prey is less accessible. But normally the

GEORGE L. MOUNTAINLION
(courtesy of Arizona–Sonora Desert Museum)

potential food supply for a mountain lion is so great, and the big cat's skill as a hunter is so sharp, that it will avoid the great hazard of raiding domestic stocks and exposing itself to human encounters. When mountain lions and people cross paths, it is normally because people have invaded the cat's territory, and not the other way around.

Partly due to the quality of the writing, and partly due to the public's fascination with *Puma concolor*, the response to George L. Mountainlion's column was overwhelming. Mail poured in. Many of the readers were children, and their letters were often addressed simply "George, Tucson, Arizona." Letters also came from adults, not only from Tucson and throughout Arizona, but from surrounding states as well.

Although the column ran in the *Arizona Daily Star* for 16 years, the original George L. Mountainlion died on March 8, 1955. George the First was buried on the museum grounds, with a handsome marble headstone commemorating him. His epitaph reads as follows:

> I FREELY GIVE ALL SIGHTS AND SOUNDS OF NATURE I HAVE KNOWN TO THOSE WHO HAVE THE GRACE TO ENJOY NOT MAN-MADE MATERIALISM BUT GOD-MADE BEAUTY
>
> THE MAGNIFICENT ARIZONA SUNSETS I HAVE WATCHED FROM MY ENCLOSURE, I BEQUEATH TO ALL WHO SEE NOT ONLY WITH THEIR EYES BUT WITH THEIR HEARTS
>
> TO HUMANS WHO ARE TIRED, WORRIED OR DISCOURAGED, I BEQUEATH THE SILENCE, MAJESTY, AND PEACE OF OUR GREAT AMERICAN DESERT.
>
> TO THOSE WHO WALK THE TRAILS, I BEQUEATH THE EARLY MORNING VOICES OF THE BIRDS, AND THE GLORY OF THE FLOWERING DESERT IN THE SPRINGTIME
>
> TO THE CHILDREN WHO HAVE ENJOYED SEEING ME, HEARING ME PURR, AND WATCHING ME TURN MY SOMERSAULTS, I OFFER THE PRECIOUS GIFT OF LAUGHTER AND JOY. THE WORLD SO NEEDS THESE THINGS
>
> AND LASTLY, I BEQUEATH MY OWN HAPPY SPIRIT, AND AFFECTION FOR OTHERS, TO ALL WHO MAY REMEMBER ME AND MY MUSEUM WHERE FOR THREE YEARS, I DID MY BEST TO SHOW PEOPLE THAT I TRULY LIKED THEM.

SOURCE: Carr, William H. *The Desert Speaks.* Tucson: The Arizona–Sonora Desert Museum, 1953–1969.

Arkansas

ANIMAL: The Running Razorback
DOB: Originally designated in 1909
DOD: Wild hogs normally live between 15 and 20 years
DESCRIPTION: The American wild hog (*Sus scrofa*), 30" high at shoulder, 300 to 400 pounds, dark brown or black.

The eyes squint closed, and the expression twists into a pained grimace of pure rage. The mouth pants half-opened, a curved tusk protruding prominently from the lower jaw, and a large drop of spittle falling backwards from the tongue. The bristled back arches skyward, and all four hoofed feet sail above the ground in an unrestrained gallop. The tail curls pretzel-like behind the rump, and a cloud of dust billows behind the racing image.

Since 1926, this has been the mascot of the University of Arkansas Running Razorbacks. Originally drawn by alumni artist Hank Hancock, this image has been used to depict the soul of the Arkansas team: independent, courageous, powerful. "Arkansas Never Quits!"

In 1909, the team name for the University of Arkansas at Fayetteville (in the northwest corner of the state) was the Cardinals. This all changed when Hugo Bezdek, a former football player at the University of Chicago under coach A.A. Stagg, came to University of Arkansas as the new football coach. Bezdeg, a Bohemian immigrant, brought several innovations to the Arkansas game, such as the forward pass and the hurry-up offense. Local legend tells how, after a 34–0 rout of Washington University in 1909, Bezdeg was heard to say that his team "fought like a herd of razorbacks." Another version of the naming story says that on a trip to Texas, a bystander greeted the arrival of the team with the comment, "Here comes the Razorbacks!" In any case, the name stuck. It was officially changed from the Cardinals in 1916, and the university team has been called the Razorbacks ever since. Not long after the name change, the traditional "calling of the hawgs" emerged as part of the ritual: "Whooo-oooo Pigs! Sooooie! Razorbacks!" Eventually a live hog was added as team mascot, wheeled out in a cage before every football game.

Razorbacks are actually domesticated hogs turned wild, or feral. Hernando de Soto, the sixteenth-century Spanish explorer, may possibly have been the first to bring hogs across Mississippi, in 1541. These animals were primarily used as a source of food for the men. Some of the pigs escaped into the wild and became as fierce and dangerous as any animal native to North America. In the 1800s, herds of swine ran wild in the Ozarks. Over the years stories have been told of wild boars weighing 300 pounds and brandishing 10-inch tusks. Sows, especially with piglets, were particularly aggressive, and may have been the principal source for the wild hogs' fiery reputation. These animals were lean and raw, cunning and courageous. When the wild hog prepared to charge, the bristles on its spine would stand up, sharp as razors — thus the name "razorback."

In the wild, hogs will travel in herds of five to fifteen animals. They are as opportunistic as they are omnivorous, eating whatever they can gather or capture: roots, grasses, berries, nuts, eggs, mice, snakes, salamanders, frogs, young birds, rabbits, and even fawns. Unlike domestic pigs, wild hogs are lean and fast, and they are much cleaner than their reputation allows.

Highly intelligent animals, domesticated hogs can be kept as pets as well as livestock. Although these animals sometimes appear fat and lazy, they can run remarkably fast if they need to, and are good swimmers. Pioneers settling in the Ozarks would allow their own domesticated hogs to run wild to find their own food. When rounding them up, the farmer would call "Whoooooooooo, Pig! Soooie!" No doubt some of the hogs decided to ignore the farmer's call and became the wild running razorbacks.

Hank Hancock came to University of Arkansas in 1921. He had illustrated his Oklahoma high school yearbook with cartoons the year before, and he continued this function for the University of Arkansas. He toyed with several versions of the Razorback — both running and standing still — over the next four years. Apparently, he drew one of his first Razorback cartoons for a man named "Crip" Hall, who is credited with originating the annual Fayetteville Homecoming. Hall eventually became Secretary of State, holding that position longer than anyone else in Arkansas history.

In 1924, Hancock took a class from art teacher Elizabeth Galbraith. Her class was based on the work of artist J. Hambridge, developed from what is called the Theory of Dynamic Symmetry. Using a combination of squares and rectangles intermingled with horizontal, vertical, and diagonal lines, this method enabled artists to convey movements that more closely resembled those of real-life models. From this method, Hancock's famous original drawing of the Running Razorback emerged.

By 1926, Hancock had graduated and was working as a commercial artist for Southwestern Engraving Company of Fort Worth, Texas. The focus of his work, not surprisingly, was illustrating high school and college yearbooks. While at Southwestern, he sent a sketch of the Running Razorback to then head football coach Francis "Smitty" Schmidt, who is credited with originating the slogan "Arkansas Never Quits." Hancock also sent the drawings to University president David W. Mullins. The drawing eventually evolved into the mascot for the University of Arkansas.

SOURCES: Hancock, Hank. *A History of Arkansas Razorbacks.* Published by the author, 1976. / Henry, Orville. "Revival of the Running Razorback." *Arkansas Gazette,* October 25, 1975.

California

ANIMAL: Humphrey
DOB: Sometime between 1981 and 1984
DOD: Unknown — probably still alive
DESCRIPTION: Pacific humpback whale (*Megaptera novaeangliae*), 45' long, 40 tons, slate gray, orange barnacles.

There were plenty of headlines in 1985 to keep San Francisco Bay Area newspaper readers occupied. That was the year the San Francisco Forty-Niners defeated the Miami Dolphins 38–16 for the Super Bowl Title; the year a great earthquake in Mexico killed more than 2000 people; the year the Night Stalker, Richard Ramirez, was captured in Los Angeles; and the year legendary filmmaker Orson Welles died. But no story captured the imagination of the bay area — and the world — like that of a Pacific humpback whale named Humphrey.

Humpback whales grow up to 45 feet long and weigh nearly 40 tons. While Humphrey's trek into the San Francisco Bay and the Sacramento Delta was an anomaly, humpback whales are commonly found along the California shore, especially off the Point Reyes area of Marin County. A great distinguishing feature of the humpback is its enormous pectoral flippers, which can grow to a length of one-third of its entire body. The humpback also has many throat grooves, which it uses to channel water when it feeds on krill. The hump for which it is named is followed closely by a small, hooked dorsal fin. If there is white on this fin — formed from years of courtship battles — the whale is likely to be a male. The blow is V-shaped, and the humpback has a series of dark nodules on its head. It is black on the back, and light on the underside.

For years, artists have depicted humpbacks and other whales as having huge, broad heads. These drawings are based on sightings of beached whales, whose heads become bloated and distended. In truth, the heads of healthy humpbacks are much more alligator-shaped, streamlined and comparatively thin.

For the most part these whales are found in the open ocean, where there is plenty of room for them to swim and breech and jump. But every once in a while, for some inexplicable reason, one of these fantastic creatures will take a detour. For 26 days in the fall of 1985, an adult humpback did just that, and the eyes of the world watched every twist and turn through the San Francisco Bay.

Humphrey was first spotted on Friday, October 11. His route took him under the Golden Gate Bridge, south of Treasure Island and near the Port of Oakland, north and west toward Angel Island; under the Richmond–San Rafael Bridge, the Benicia Bridge, and the Carquinez Bridge through the delta and up the Sacramento River, and then back again. The entire sojourn covered very nearly 200 miles of the San Francisco Bay and the Sacramento Delta.

It is hard to tell why Humphrey headed up the Sacramento River. Scientists have concluded simply that he must have taken a "wrong turn" and became lost. One illustrated Humphrey's predicament by comparing it to "walking into a dark cave with a lot of passages," pointing out "how difficult it would be to find your way out." In any case, when Humphrey swam far beyond San Pablo Bay — the northern portion of San Francisco Bay — and northeast up into the Sacramento River, he entered a particularly shallow and muddy eddy of the river called Shag Slough. As Humphrey made his way up toward the slough, several problems confronted him. Aside from the problems of space, the narrower the passageway became, the greater likelihood for direct contact with human beings and their watercraft. Although, by all accounts, people were very cautious and considerate, there was always a chance that some lunatic might get in the way and cause considerable harm to himself or the whale.

Another problem was the shallowness of the water. The great weight of humpback whales requires a great deal of displacement of water to provide buoyancy; without that buoyancy, the whale can crush itself with its own great weight.

The greatest danger, however, was the fresh water. Humpback whales require salt water to live, for fresh water tends to seep into the whale's body, which becomes waterlogged. In addition, the fresher the water, the less likely Humphrey would be able to find his favorite salt-water food, krill. Experts estimated Humphrey could survive perhaps ten days in the river, after which he would very likely drown or starve.

When Humphrey first made his way up the river, officials and the public found it to be an amusing oddity, all the time expecting that the whale would eventually turn seaward. Spectators lined up on the sides of the river — traveling from miles around — to catch sight of this spectacular mammal. But as he continued northward, amusement turned to concern and then to fear. When Humphrey swam through the pillars of the footbridge on Shag Slough, everyone began to understand that the whale was in trouble.

Humphrey began to look ill, and he found the maneuvering in Shag Slough to be difficult. Time was short, and if he was unable to change his course soon, the whale would certainly die. Coast Guard officers and scientists began employing several methods to head Humphrey back under the bridge and out toward the ocean. They created loud noises behind the whale to scare him back toward the bridge. On the other side of the bridge, recorded whale sounds were broadcast to lure Humphrey southward. At first the methods worked. Humphrey began swimming back toward the bridge. But then he stopped, apparently unable to navigate through the narrow spaces among the bridge posts. Humphrey seemed to become angry and flustered, rolling and thrashing — which, of course, would only tire him further. A crane was brought in to dig a deeper trench through which the whale could swim, and to remove old pilings and debris that further blocked his path.

Finally, after three days in Shag Slough, at the urgings of the noises, Humphrey tried to make his way past the bridge. Momentarily, he seemed to be stuck among the posts, and for several terrible minutes spectators feared he would be drowned. But then Humphrey rolled his great form onto its side and practically wiggled from underneath the bridge.

The gathered throngs cheered as Humphrey swam back out toward the bay. The coast guard flanked his front and rear, continuing the noises, trying to insure as much as possible that the whale found its way back home. After momentary stops to rest and play along the way, on November 5, 1985, Humphrey floated back under the Golden Gate Bridge, and back to the Pacific Ocean.

SOURCES: *San Francisco Chronicle*, October 11, 1985, through November 5, 1985. / Tokuda, Wendy, and Hall, Richard. *Humphrey, the Lost Whale*. Union City, Calif.: Heian, 1986.

ANIMAL: Koko
DOB: July 4, 1971
DESCRIPTION: Western lowland gorilla (*Gorilla gorilla*), approximately 5' tall, 180 pounds, black coat.

The relationship that has historically existed between humans and animals is less an actual relationship than a coexistence. Obviously, animals and humans have interacted and affected each other since the dawn of time, but without the one element that is essential for a relationship: the mutual exchange of ideas that constitutes real communication. Certainly, humans have long fantasized about the ability to communicate with animals. But for the most part, human beings have simply given orders, to which animals have responded in a positive or negative fashion. So much for communication, and so much for a relationship.

Then along came a western lowland gorilla named Koko. Koko was born on July 4, 1971, at the San Francisco Zoo, the offspring of Jackie and Bwana. Her formal name was Hanabiko, which is Japanese for "fireworks child," but everyone called her Koko. Life for Koko would have been pretty much the same as for every other gorilla raised in captivity, were it not for a Stanford University graduate student of developmental psychology named Francine Patterson. Patterson's fascination with the idea of communicating with animals spearheaded what came to be known as the Koko Project. Since 1972, Dr. Patterson and Koko have been learning to communicate with one another using American Sign Language. Under Patterson's tutelage, Koko has learned to communicate in rhyme, to tell jokes, even to lie.

When Patterson met Koko, the gorilla had been ill with shigella enteritis. She had become severely malnourished and dehydrated and had to be isolated from her mother and the other gorillas. This isolation may have been key to Patterson's selection of Koko, since Koko would have already been used to separation from the other gorillas, and development away from the gorilla community would not be as traumatic for her as it might for other gorilla children.

Although Patterson had yet to be granted permission to work with the gorilla, she began to visit Koko in recovery every day. At first, Koko was extremely wary of Patterson, and even bit her when she tried to pick Koko up. Slowly but surely, however, Koko came to trust Patterson, and as they spent more time together, an intimate bond began to form. This bond became integral to the success of Project Koko.

American Sign Language does not rely on finger-spelling of words, but rather on gestures that convey complete ideas. For example, "drink" is conveyed with a clenched fist, thumb extended and brought up to the lips. Koko's venture into American Sign Language began with the signs for "drink," "food," and "more." Patterson used these signs whenever Koko ate, and she instructed the zoo assistants who worked in Koko's nursery to use the signs as well. Whenever Koko was presented with food, it was accompanied by the ASL sign for food; whenever she was given drink, the "drink" sign was shown with it; when Koko was given more food, the assistants signed "more."

This repetition continued for about a month. Then, one morning, as Patterson was preparing Koko's snack, the gorilla formed the sign for "food" with her hands. As Patterson watched in amazement, Koko made the sign again. Patterson was ecstatic, and the gorilla, apparently sharing in her friend's excitement, joy, and sense of accomplishment, put a bucket on her head and began running happily about the room. The human and the gorilla had crossed an important bridge: They had learned to communicate an idea.

Patterson's attempts to communicate with a gorilla at first met with much skepticism from colleagues. Most of them assumed that a chimpanzee would be a better choice for such a project. Gorillas, in comparison to chimpanzees, were considered dim-witted, slow, and dangerous, because of their enormous strength and relatively unknown character. The gorilla's shy, retiring ways were evidently mistaken for a lack of intelligence, while the chimpanzee's gregarious nature — it often seems to enjoy the company of humans — was accepted as a sign of superior intellect.

Over the years, however, Koko's intelligence and resourcefulness have made themselves obvious. At the age of four years, the gorilla had a vocabulary of more than 161 words, and by five years it had passed 350 words. Today her vocabulary is well over 600 words. But more important than Koko's simple accumulation of words has been her ability to communicate about the world from the gorilla's point of view.

For example, during one conversation about death, Koko was asked where gorillas go when they die. Koko responded by signing, "Comfortable hole bye," exhibiting none of the trepidation which often accompanies a human conversation about death. When asked where baby gorillas come from, Koko signed her own name; when asked where in Koko babies come from, Koko pointed to her abdomen. Other conversations have included such topics as gorilla fears, the differences and similarities between humans and gorillas, and the use of sign language itself.

In 1974, Patterson, Koko, and Dr. Ronald Cohn (documenting photographer for Project Koko) moved to a trailer and compound at Stanford University, where Project Koko was continued. In 1979, they all moved to a farm in Woodside, some ten miles north of Stanford. Along the way a male gorilla named Michael was acquired as a companion to Koko. In 1984, Koko was given a pet, a cat she named "All Ball." And of course, the breakthrough work of Koko and Patterson has been the focus of worldwide media attention. *Science, Reader's Digest,* and *National Geographic* have all featured articles on their compelling story, as have the television and radio news media throughout the world.

Project Koko continues in the hills of Woodside, California, to this day. Although there have been other communication projects with apes — most notably, the work of Allan and Beatrice Gardner with a female chimpanzee named Washoe, which provided much inspiration for Dr. Patterson's work — Project Koko is the longest ongoing study of language capabilities in apes. As the project continues to unfold, the relationship of Dr. Patterson and Koko continues to grow — as a real relationship, based on their appreciation for one another's point of view.

SOURCES: Linden, Eugene, and Patterson, Francine. *The Education of Koko.* New York: Holt, Rinehart, and Winston, 1981. / Patterson, Francine. *Koko's Story.* New York: Scholastic, 1987.

Colorado

ANIMAL: Old Mose
DOB: Probably 1860s
DOD: 1904
DESCRIPTION: Grizzly bear (*Ursus arctos*), cinnamon brown with silver tips, 10' 4" long, approximately 1200 pounds.

The largest bear ever killed in the State of Colorado, according to the *Denver Post* in 1904, was a nineteenth century Grizzly named "Old Mose." Old Mose was named, apparently, for the way he would mosey into a miner's camp, scare everyone from the place, help himself to whatever food he could find, and then mosey out again.

Old Mose measured ten feet, four inches long, and weighed more than 1200 pounds. His paw tracks measured ten inches in diameter, and his claws alone were five inches long. Eventually he lost two of the toes of the right front paw to a steel trap; Old Mose had freed himself from the trap by chewing those two toes off. He was so strong that he was credited with lifting a dead cow out of a three-foot-deep trap with one paw.

Between 1878 and 1903, Old Mose carried on his reign of terror over south-central Colorado. From Leadville to Monte Vista to Gunnison and Canon City — an area of about 30,000 square miles — Old Mose is blamed for the killing of more than 800 head of cattle valued at more than $30,000. Ranchers and hunters pursued him relentlessly throughout those years, and one newspaper claimed he was

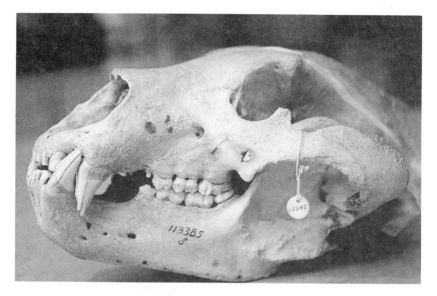

THE SKULL OF OLD MOSE
(courtesy of Museum of Vertebrate Zoology, U.C. Berkeley)

shot through and through times without number, baited with every device and cunning known to the trapper; chased by the demon posses of cowboys and ranchers bent upon his extermination, and in all this he has met them with superior generalship, cunning unexcelled, knowledge supreme.

Inevitably, as encounters with Old Mose increased, some men lost their lives. The deaths of three humans are credited to Old Mose.

The first was a deer hunter named Jake Radcliff. While trooping through the forests near Badger Creek, he inadvertently stumbled onto Old Mose's den. He was found later by other hunters. He had broken bones in his legs and ankles. His cheek was torn with a furious claw, and he was bitten across the entirety of the back of his head, his scalp nearly torn off. He died en route to the town of Fairplay, unable to withstand the loss of blood, exposure, exhaustion, and excruciating pain.

A second victim's skeleton was found on Cameron Mountain, lying beside a rusted old rifle. The remains were identified as belonging to James Asher, and the death was attributed to Old Mose due to the apparent injuries. A third corpse belonged to an unidentified cowboy, whose bones, boots, and spurs were found north of Guffey.

It is almost always the case with any large predator that casualties among humans increase when contact with the predator grows more frequent. Humans have continually encroached on what was once strictly hunting territory for grizzlies and other predators, developing the wilderness into farms and

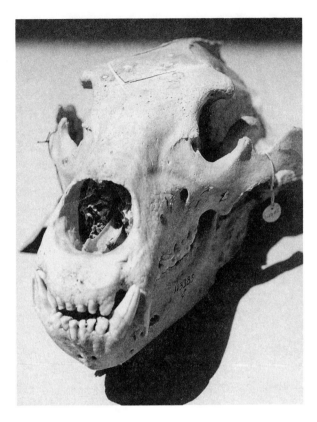

THE SKULL OF OLD MOSE
(courtesy of Museum of Vertebrate Zoology, U.C. Berkeley)

communities. The grizzly bear's common habitat once stretched from Alaska and the Yukon Territories down to Mexico, from the Pacific Ocean to the Great Plains. Today, the grizzly has been eliminated from California, and all but eliminated from North America. Only in a handful of national parks, as well as in Alaska and parts of British Columbia and Alberta, does the great grizzled bear continue to survive.

On April 30, 1904, a hunter named James W. Anthony from Boise, Idaho, brought the life of Old Mose to an end. Accompanied by another hunter and eight hunting dogs, Anthony tracked Old Mose to Black Mountain. He shot the bear five times, the last time between the eyes as it was charging. It took seven men to pack Old Mose back down the mountain. Anthony displayed the huge carcass at Wright and Morgan Market in Canon City, and 3,000 astonished viewers traveled there to gawk and wonder at Old Mose.

After Anthony died, the skull and hide of Old Mose were willed to the Museum of Vertebrate Zoology in Berkeley, California, where they remain today, objects of study for graduates and post-graduates of zoology from the University of California. Dr. Ellsworth Lancaster, a professor of psychology and neuroanatomy from Colorado College in Colorado Springs, studied the remains of Old Mose's brain. From his study he drew a conclusion that is no doubt true of most large carnivores that have been scorned and persecuted by humans:

> This bear did not reason, did not love or hate, probably and was mild and peaceable if left alone. If frightened or injured or hungry, his instincts said run, crush, or kill.

SOURCE: Shirley, Gayle C. *Four Legged Legends of Colorado.* Helena, Mont.: Falcon, 1994.

Connecticut

ANIMAL: Jumbo
DOB: 1865
DOD: September 1885
DESCRIPTION: African elephant (*Elephas africanas*), 11' at shoulder, 6.5 tons.

The most famous animal of Connecticut is quite likely the most famous elephant in history, probably the most famous circus animal in history, perhaps even the most famous animal of all. Everything about Jumbo was jumbo, and his impact on Connecticut, the Eastern Seaboard, England, the English language, the American Public, and entertainment in general was equally colossal.

Jumbo was a male African elephant who stood more than 11 feet tall and weighed in excess of 13,000 pounds. He ate more than 300 pounds of food a day, washing it down with five buckets of water. The very word "jumbo" has been assimilated into the American parlance to mean anything gigantic or, according to Webster, "a very large specimen of its kind." Even today, beer, soft drink, pretzels, and peanuts, all come in "jumbo" size. This association with extravagance is a fitting tribute to an animal who was once the primary attraction of premier American showman and propagandist Phineus T. Barnum.

Jumbo was captured as a baby by Hamran Arabs in 1865. The Arabs sold him to a Bavarian named Johann Schmidt who, in turn, sold it to the Jardin des Plantes in Paris. At the time, the elephant who was to become Jumbo stood only four feet tall. Disappointed, the director of the Jardin traded the baby elephant to the London Zoological Gardens for a rhinoceros.

In 1882, when the London Zoological Garden sold Jumbo to P.T. Barnum

JUMBO
(lithograph courtesy of The New-York Historical Society)

for $10,000, a wave of melancholy swept through England. Jumbo had become a great favorite in that country. Britain's children, who had spent 17 years riding on the beast's back, wept openly in the streets. The English Parliament, and even Queen Victoria herself, joined in the plea for the London Zoo to renege on the contract, but to no avail. Jumbo the Elephant crossed the Atlantic Ocean aboard the *Assyrian Monarch*, arriving in New York on Easter Sunday.

The United States was more than ready to welcome an attraction such as Jumbo, as well as any other phenomenon Barnum was willing to present — or to exploit, as some would say. The country was enjoying the fruits of a post-war industrial revolution, and leisure activities such as baseball, harness racing, and circuses were finding their ways to the masses. America was also developing a new fascination with animal life, spawned by vigorous interest in the writings of Charles Darwin. Jumbo could not have arrived at a more advantageous time — especially for P.T. Barnum.

Jumbo was presented to the American public with the usual Barnum flare. One advertisement proclaimed, "His trunk is the size of an adult crocodile, his tail is as big as a cow's leg, and he made footprints in the sands of time resembling an indentation as if a very fat man had fallen off a very tall building." Thousands of children rode Jumbo's back, and Jumbo products — ranging from hats to cigars — sold by the score.

For the three years Jumbo lived in the United States, his winter quarters were at Waldemere, P.T. Barnum's fabulous estate at Bridgeport, Connecticut. While residing in Bridgeport, Jumbo provided the services of a beast of burden for the Barnum estate.

It all came to a tragic end in September of 1885. At 9:00 on September

15, the circus was being loaded for departure from a performance at St. Thomas, Ontario, Canada. An attendant was leading Jumbo to his private car with his fellow performer, Tom Thumb (a baby elephant used to emphasize Jumbo's great girth). Suddenly an unscheduled freight train roared around the corner, headed straight for the elephants. The impact hurled Tom Thumb aside, and Jumbo incurred the brunt of the crash. The collision crushed Jumbo's massive skull, while smashing and derailing the engine and two cars. Jumbo rolled over to one side, and in a few moments, he died.

Barnum was never to find an attraction to replace Jumbo the Elephant. Barnum once estimated Jumbo had been seen by nine million Americans, easily the greatest single feature of Barnum's many great shows. Although the showman tried to minimize the loss, it was clear that the Barnum and Bailey Circus would never fully recover. As it turned out, neither would Barnum. He went into semi-retirement at Waldemere soon afterward, and died in 1891.

SOURCES: Harris, Neal. *Humbug: The Art of P. T. Barnum.* Boston: Little, Brown, 1973. / Saxon, A.H. *P. T. Barnum: The Man and the Legend.* New York: Columbia University Press, 1989.

Delaware

ANIMAL: The Blue Hen chicken (*Gallus gallus*)
DESCRIPTION: Approximately 12" tall, blue-grey feathers, strongly hooked tail feathers, elongated and linear rump feathers, reddish nude and wattled throat, reddish fleshy comb on forehead.

During the American Revolutionary War, Captain Jonathan Caldwell commanded a military company from Kent County, Delaware, which encompasses the capital city of Dover. Captain Caldwell's company was attached to the regiment of Colonel John Haslett. The Delaware company fought bravely and fiercely at Haslett's side through several campaigns. These included the crushing defeat at the hands of General Sir William Howe at White Plains, New York, in October 1776, and the colonial Christmas victory under General George Washington at Trenton, New Jersey.

During the course of the war, the Delaware troops often entertained themselves between battles with engagements in cockfighting. The cocks Captain Caldwell procured for his troops were reputed to be of the famous Blue Hen breed. Caldwell's men would pit the Blue Hen cocks against rival troops' chickens. These roosters fought with such valor and ferocity that their fights became famous throughout the colonial army. The troop itself was compared to these fighting cocks and soon came to be known as "The Blue Hen's Chickens."

The Blue Hen chicken is not actually a separate breed of fowl. It is, instead, a color variation of the Old English game chicken. These birds came over with the colonists from England in the seventeenth century and have been a staple of American agriculture ever since. These chickens are well thought of for their meat, their eggs, and apparently, their fighting ability.

Cockfighting was introduced to America by the British colonists, and where there was cockfighting, there was almost always drinking and gambling. That is why cockfighting was officially banned by Puritan New England, while it flourished in colonial states from New York to Georgia. The popularity of the sport continued through the nineteenth century, but public sentiment against cruelty to animals, alcohol, and gambling eventually brought legal cockfighting to an end. Today, cockfighting is illegal in most states, but it is also practiced in most states.

The cockpit in which these bizarre contests take place is commonly 16 to 18 feet in circumference, surrounded by walls 16 to 24 inches high. Cocks are thrown into the pit, where they gouge and peck each other with beaks and feet and spurs (small, sharp bones which grow just above the feet). To add to the grotesque spectacle, cocks often wear artificial spurs made of iron, gold, silver, or bronze. The natural spurs are filed down and then replaced by the metal spurs, which enable the fighting cocks to disembowel each other at a stroke. Cocks fight until one cannot or will not fight any longer.

Despite the gore — or more likely because of it — some estimate that cockfighting is a multimillion dollar business.

Cockfighting has been practiced throughout history in virtually every corner of the world. Although illegal through much of North America and Europe, cockfighting is still practiced legally in many parts of the world. The cock has traditionally been the symbol of courage, fertility, virility, and the sun, and has been adopted as the symbol for warriors throughout the centuries.

The symbolism has not been lost on Delaware. Ever since the Revolution, the Blue Hen has found itself enmeshed in the history of the First State. On May 4, 1861, a company of soldiers assembled from Delaware for the Civil War was also named Blue Hens' Chickens. In 1910, at a ceremony honoring the newly commissioned U.S.S. *Delaware*, a pair of Blue Hen chickens was presented in honor of the vessel. The Blue Hen motif has been used in numerous Delaware political campaigns and state publications, and the state flag is flown with a model of the Blue Hen's fighting cock on top of the flagpole. The Blue Hen chicken was adopted as the University of Delaware mascot, and finally, the Blue Hen was recognized as the state bird through a law enacted by the state legislature on April 14, 1939.

SOURCES: Shearer, Benjamin F., and Shearer, Barbara S. *State Names, Seals, Flags, and Symbols*. Westport, Conn.: Greenwood, 1994.

District of Columbia

ANIMAL: Hsing-Hsing and Ling-Ling
DOB: Hsing-Hsing, April 1971; Ling-Ling, May 1970
DOD: Ling-Ling, 1992; Hsing-Hsing is alive
DESCRIPTION: Species: Great pandas (*Ailuropoda melanoleuca*), soft black and white coat, approximately 6' long; Ling-Ling, 224 pounds, Hsing-Hsing, 203 pounds.

The most famous animal in the District of Columbia is actually a pair of animals.

The death of Ling-Ling (meaning "cute little girl"), the female giant panda, meant more to Washington, D.C., than the passing of most politicians who have inhabited the city. Not only was she more reliable, and infinitely more adorable, but she — with her mate, Hsing-Hsing (meaning "bright star") — had come to symbolize what was once thought impossible: a cooperative relationship between the People's Republic of China and the United States of America.

In 1972, president Richard Milhous Nixon was able to attain something that had eluded every other United States president: a diplomatic visit to the People's Republic of China. As a gift from the People's Republic, in exchange for two musk oxen, Nixon brought back the pandas Ling-Ling and Hsing-Hsing, soon to become the most famous zoo animals in the world.

The world has been in love with the giant panda ever since it was discovered in 1869 by Jesuit missionary Pere Armand David. It is soft, furry, and pleasantly colored. Though large and comparatively powerful, it is generally harmless, amusing, and lovable. Sometimes linked biologically with raccoons, other times with bears, the giant panda is like no other beast in the world — especially in its effect upon the human heart.

Predictably, from the moment the pair of pandas arrived at the National Zoological Park in Washington on April 16, 1972, the commercial response was astounding. Toy pandas, pandas mugs, panda posters, and other paraphernalia flooded the shops of merchants throughout the city and beyond. A Chinese restaurant in the city was named "China Panda." In January of 1973, a perfume company proclaimed Ling-Ling and Hsing-Hsing "Valentines of the Year."

Celebrities, statespersons, and ordinary citizens flocked to the Panda House to watch the prized residents. Nixon's secretary of state, Henry Kissinger, was at least one regular visitor; he was apparently fond of visiting the National Zoo to watch the pandas have their breakfast.

Those breakfasts, by the way, were prodigious. In their native habitat, the pandas would eat bamboo shoots, flowers, vines, grass, and even small animals.

LING-LING AND HSING-HSING
(courtesy of Jessie Cohen, National Zoological Park Smithsonian Institution)

At the zoo, their diets were supplemented with rice, fruits, vegetables, and for a particularly special treat, honey. Pandas have very specialized forefeet, which they use like hands to grasp their food. It is understandable why Kissinger — and so many other people — found watching the pair at mealtime so fascinating.

The ultimate hope, of course, was that Hsing-Hsing and Ling-Ling would become father and mother — something that had never been successfully attempted outside the Republic of China. Even within China, successful captive breeding has occurred only ten times, and three of those successes were through artificial insemination.

Many of the obstacles to the reproductive process involved complications of timing. Imagine the difficulty of finding a time when Ling-Ling was in heat, Hsing-Hsing was rutting, and all other conditions — the animals' maturity, their health, their adaptation to their environment, even the weather — were favorable. Adding to the difficulty was the solitary nature of pandas, which tends to keep them isolated from each other.

Nonetheless, zoo officials tried several times to arrange the commingling of Hsing-Hsing and Ling-Ling. In desperation, the keepers even tried to mate Ling-Ling with the London Zoo's Chia-Chia, to no avail. Finally, Ling-Ling gave birth to five cubs sired by Hsing-Hsing, but all died very young due to immunity abnormalities.

So, for more than 20 years, Hsing-Hsing and Ling-Ling ruled the National Zoological Garden roost by themselves. Then, on the morning of December 30, 1992, Ling-Ling was found dead of heart failure in her cage at the age of 23.

Almost immediately, and every day for many weeks, cards, letters, and drawings arrived at the zoo, mourning the death of Ling-Ling. From adults and children who had been captivated over the years by the giant pandas, these messages paid tribute to Ling-Ling and her mate, and to the harmonious possibilities they represented.

SOURCES: "Bye-Bye, Ling Ling." *People*, January 18, 1993. P. 61. / Collins, Larry R., and Page, James K., Jr. *Ling-Ling and Hsing-Hsing: Year of the Panda*. New York: Doubleday, 1973.

Florida

ANIMAL: Flipper (a.k.a. Suzy, Patty, Kathy, or others)
DOB: Approximately 1960
DOD: Approximately 1968
DESCRIPTION: Bottlenose dolphin (*Tursiops truncatus*), 12' long, 400
    pounds.

Between 1964 and 1967, the theme song for NBC's "Flipper" was a popular anthem for families throughout America. The show, which aired on Saturday nights, without a doubt made Flipper the most popular animal in Florida. "Flipper" was produced by Ivan Tors and costarred Brian Kelly as Ranger Porter Ricks, Luke Halpin as Sandy Ricks, and Tommy Norden as Bud Ricks. More than 90 episodes were filmed in Miami and the Bahamas, depicting the Ricks family with their redoubtable dolphin, Flipper.

The show was perfect entertainment for a child growing up in the sixties. One of the best things about "Flipper" was its predictability. Not only did the same theme song open and close each episode, but each show involved familiar elements in a sequence one could always count on:

    * One of the Ricks boys — usually Bud — gets into some kind of trouble, and the other Ricks boy — usually Sandy — tries to bail him out, but also get into trouble.

    * A number of beautiful underwater scenes depict Flipper in his domain.

    * Somewhere within the story, one of the Ricks family — usually Bud or Sandy, but sometimes Porter — engages in a conversation with Flipper, with perfect comprehension on both sides.

    * Porter Ricks, fatherly scowl upon his face, metes out some form of punishment to his remorseful sons.

    * In the climax, Flipper rescues everyone.

Bottlenose dolphins are Cetaceans, members of the family that includes whales and porpoises. These dolphins can grow to 12 feet long, and weigh as much as 400 pounds. They are highly intelligent and animated creatures. They eat live fish, and communicate and navigate by means of an intricate sonar system. Dolphins are incredibly swift and powerful animals, yet gentle to the extreme. There is no known report of a dolphin purposely injuring a human being; in fact, there have been many stories since the dawn of time of wild dolphins helping and even saving people. Dolphin trainers seem to count on this natural gentleness and helpfulness. Still, what is gentle for a 400-pound dolphin can be hazardous for a human being. As when working with any essentially wild animal in an unnatural setting, trainers for the "Flipper" series exercised the utmost caution and flexibility when working with the dolphins.

The original dolphin for the series was actually named Suzy, and she was discovered at Miami's Seaquarium, under the direction of diver and trainer Richard O'Barry. For the first year of the series, she seemed to work well within the constructs of the filming. Like all the dolphins, Suzie was rewarded with live fish for her cooperation. As time went on, Suzie became more spoiled, and more impatient for her rewards. She would splash water or push people with her snout if she did not get her fish right away. Although she never hurt anyone, she scared several of the actors and crew members. She was eventually phased out of the show. By the end of the series, in 1968, she had been sold to a European circus. She later died of pneumonia.

Suzy was followed in the title role by Patty, then by Kathy, Squirt, and by other female dolphins. Females were used because they tended to be less aggressive than male dolphins. O'Barry handled all of the dolphins used in the "Flipper" series.

In his book about the series, O'Barry neatly summarized the "Flipper" effect:

    Flipper was an illusion, an elaborate fabrication, the work of hundreds of talented people who came thousands of miles and spent thousands of dollars, all to create the legend of a fabulous creature, a creature combining both actual and imaginary delphoid powers with that of a family pet specially blessed — as all of them are when we love them — with human intelligence. That Flipper is more imaginary than real can be said of anyone who presents himself to the public. Cary Grant used to say that even he wished he could be Cary Grant, the Cary Grant portrayed on films.

Flipper was essentially the "Lassie of the Sea," and the song's claim that no one was smarter than Flipper seemed to be the running theme of the show. However, despite the heroic illusion created for the main character — not to mention the corny plots and questionable acting — Flipper performed a valuable service by raising an awareness of dolphins and marine life in general among the American public. Members of the television audience were able — many for the first time — to discover the "world full of wonder" under the sea, and became familiar with the intelligence, power, and grace of the Bottlenose dolphin. The audience also came to learn about other forms of marine life, particularly those indigenous to the southeastern tip of the United States.

The show, of course, was immensely popular, and still can be seen in reruns throughout the country. Luke Halpin was thrust into the teen heart-throb spotlight in the role of Sandy Ricks, and even today he and Tommy Norden receive occasional fan mail from viewers still enthralled with the show. When the series swam off into syndication in 1968, "Flipper" was the name attributed to a series of dolphins who would — and still do to this day — perform at Seaquarium.

SOURCES: O'Barry, Richard. *Behind the Dolphin Smile.* Chapel Hill, N.C.: Algonquin, 1988. *People*, July 19, 1993. Pp. 78–79.

Georgia

ANIMAL: Willie B.
DOB: 1958
DESCRIPTION: Western lowland gorilla (*Gorilla gorilla*), black, coat with silver tint, 6' tall, 420 pounds, arm span: 8' 4", neck: 40", chest: 62".

In 1958, a young male western lowland gorilla was captured by an animal dealer in Africa. The dealer spent the next three years raising the gorilla, then brought the animal to the Atlanta zoo in 1961. The gorilla quickly captured the hearts of zoo visitors around Georgia and beyond. He was given the name Willie B., after the former mayor of Atlanta, William B. Hartsfield (best known for introducing the cast of *Gone with the Wind* to the residents of Atlanta on December 12, 1939).

The western lowland gorilla is found in the tropical rainforests of Nigeria,

WILLIE B. THE GORILLA
(courtesy of Atlanta Zoo)

the Cameroons, Gabon, equitorial Guinea, Ghana, and the Central African Republic. In 1958, the estimated population of these gorillas was between 10,000 and 20,000 in the wild.

For 28 years after his arrival, Willie B. was the lone gorilla at the Atlanta Zoo. He would entertain the patrons by swinging about his cage in the Primate House on a hanging truck tire. He would make faces at the visitors, and watch a television set placed inside the Primate House.

And he would eat: Willie B. regularly consumes five and a half pounds of produce per day. This includes oranges, bananas, and other fruits, celery, sweet potatoes, broccoli, collard greens, bamboo branches, and a zoo specialty called primate nuggets, containing various nutrients important to growing gorillas. Willie B. tops each day with a glass of his favorite drink: milk.

Willie B. quickly became one of the most popular attractions at the Atlanta

Zoo. People would crowd about the Primate House to watch and marvel at this beast that is so much like humans, but hairier, wilder, heavier, and oh ... so much stronger!

It may be the legendary strength of gorillas — and the fantasies it inspires of having such strength oneself — that so fascinates the human mind. Though the gorilla is actually a timid, retiring, and gentle creature, stories of its prodigious power have defined the image of the gorilla for most of humanity. There is no doubt that its strength is amazing. Gorillas have been known to twist truck tires into figure eights. There are stories of gorillas wrenching rifles from the grips of hunters, bending the barrels in half with their hands, and beating the hapless hunters to death with the destroyed weapons; of seizing an adult man, taking a leg in each hand, and tearing the man in half; of lifting 600-pound cage doors like toys. In truth, due to their retiring nature, it is doubtful that anyone has ever witnessed a gorilla's full power.

In the early 1960s, zoos were not the sophisticated facilities that are being developed today. The needs and adaptability of the animals were considered secondarily to the convenience of the zoo patrons. The environment of the animals received relatively little consideration; ensuring that the animals had enough to eat and were reasonably clean was regarded as sufficient.

By the 1980s, the concept of zoos had radically changed. Perhaps because they became breeding grounds for many of the world's most endangered creatures, zoological gardens began to be designed with the needs of the animals in mind. Efforts were made to construct habitats that closely resembled native homelands — a far cry from the four gray walls and iron bars that so typified the zoos of decades past.

The Atlanta Zoo was no exception. Founded in 1889 and one of the ten oldest United States zoos in continuous operation, it was named one of *Good Housekeeping* magazine's ten best zoos in 1994. In 1985, in keeping with the new attitude towards zoos and their animals, the Atlanta Zoo began a multi-million-dollar reconstruction. Part of the reconstruction was the opening of the Ford African Rain Forest in 1988, which provided a habitat for Willie B. that greatly resembled the Central African forests in which he was born.

In 1989, gorillas from (nearby) Yerkes Regional Primate Research Center of Emory University moved into the Ford African Rain Forest. For the first time, Willie B. had other gorillas with which to interact. Socialization among the gorillas commenced successfully. Willie B. began mating with females within the group, and a social order, complete with rituals and hierarchies, began to develop among the gorillas.

Socialization took a decidedly new twist when a 29-year-old female gorilla named Choomba arrived from Yerkes Center. Willie B. socialized particularly well with Choomba, and by 1993, Choomba became pregnant with Willie B.'s first offspring. On Feb. 8, 1994, Kudzu was born.

Willie B. is now 36, quite old for an animal with an average life span of

40 years. He continues his reign as monarch of the Ford African Rain Forest and ambassador from the Atlanta Zoo.

SOURCES: Atlanta Zoo, Public Relations Department. / Willoughby, David P. *All About Gorillas*. London: A.S. Barnes, 1978. Pp. 46–55, 151–155.

Hawaii

ANIMAL: The Nene

DESCRIPTION: Nene or Hawaiian goose (*Branta sandvicensis*), 23" to 28" long, black face, crown, and nape, buff cheeks, white throat and neck, grayish torso.

Many of the hazards facing the fauna of an island can be attributed to one particular characteristic: isolation. An isolated environment may be a paradise for the species it supports, but such a paradise is extremely vulnerable to outside influences. Species growing up in island communities often do so in the presence of few or no major predators. If a disease or predator is introduced from the outside, the community is very often decimated, having developed no defense with which to protect itself.

Many islands were originally portions of continents that broke off from the mainland. In such a case, an island often takes members of the mainland ecosystem with it. These species often evolve special abilities or characteristics as adaptations to their new environment. For volcanic islands, however, the situation is different. Building out of the sea floor, there is no indigenous animal life accompanying this development. Whatever animals eventually come to inhabit these islands have migrated from other lands. These communities can be especially vulnerable to the changes in their environment. Such is the case of the state bird of Hawaii.

It is believed that when Captain James Cook landed in the Hawaiian Islands in 1778, the population of the nene, or Hawaiian goose, was more than 25,000. Today, the nene, the Hawaiian state bird, remains one of the world's rarest geese — though captive breeding programs have prevented its becoming one of the world's extinct geese.

The nene's demise commenced with the arrival of Cook to the Hawaiian Islands, then called the Sandwich Islands (after the Earl of Sandwich of eighteenth century England). The destruction began with sandalwood logging in nesting areas, and continued with the introduction of foreign species to the islands. Cook and the Europeans who followed brought cats, pigs, and dogs, many of which turned feral and found the placid nene to be easy prey. Of particular consequence was the introduction of the mongoose, originally intended to reduce the rat population (which was also introduced by the Europeans).

THE NENE
(courtesy of Hawaii Division of Forestry and Wildlife)

The mongoose devoured the eggs of the Nene and drove the species further toward extinction.

The word "nene" means "sit together and talk," and the Hawaiian goose is indeed a sociable bird. Because it had no natural enemies on the islands, the geese were very tame, and thus easy targets for hunters. Hunting parties would come back with muleloads of geese. A market for salted nene developed in California with the advent of the Gold Rush and the arrival of hungry forty-niners.

The drive toward extinction continued through the late nineteenth and early twentieth centuries. By the 1950s, fewer than 30 of the birds remained alive in the wild. Alarmed, Hawaii declared the nene a protected species and began a captive breeding program. Of particular note was the success of the Wildfowl Trust of England, headed by Sir Peter Scott. Starting with three birds sent from Hawaii in 1950, the Wildfowl Trust ultimately returned more than 200 geese to the Hawaiian Islands. In 1957, the nene was declared the state bird.

By the 1960s, more than 800 birds had been hatched, but the wild population continues to struggle. In 1994, it was estimated that fewer than 500 remained in the wild in Hawaii, with perhaps 2000 living in domestication on ranches and private grounds in Hawaii and around the world. Domestically raised geese are regularly reintroduced into the wild.

The nene is believed to have evolved from the very migratory and common Canada Goose (*Branta canadensis*), to which it bears a resemblance. The nene is a beautiful goose, with black face and head, buff-colored cheeks, and whitish throat. It lives in dry, volcanic lava fields, 1000 feet or so above sea level, primarily on the island of Hawaii, on the slopes of Mauna Kea, Mauna Loa, and Hualalai. On Maui, it was recently introduced at Halaeakala Crater.

The nene has developed semi-webbed, long-toed feet, which enable it to climb steep volcanic slopes. Though the nene rarely swims in its natural habitat — which rarely contains substantial bodies of water — it is known to swim freely when domesticated. The nene feeds on grass, herbs, seeds, and berries. It is non-migratory, although it is believed at one time to have migrated between the islands of Maui and Hawaii, some 80 miles by air.

With its wild population leveling off and its domestic population increasing, the nene is a monument to captive breeding, suggesting hope for species such as the California condor and the whooping crane. Certainly, without these efforts, the Hawaiian goose would have disappeared down the path of the passenger pigeon, the dodo, and the great auk.

SOURCES: Clark, Hugh. "Volcano Areas Too Close to Protect Nene Goslings." *The Honolulu Advertiser*, October 2, 1994. P. A6. / Soothill, Eric, and Whitehead, Peter. *Wildfowl of the World*. London: Blandford, 1988. Pp.84–85. / Todd, Frank S. *Waterfowl: Ducks, Geese, and Swans of the World*. San Diego: Sea World, 1979. Pp. 323–325.

Idaho

ANIMAL: Sharlie
DOB: Unknown
DOD: Unknown
DESCRIPTION: Sturgeon (*Acipenseridae huso*) or serpent? Size and appearance vary according to story.

In 1920, lumberjacks from the Brown Tie and Lumber Mill were working at the northern end of Idaho's Payette Lake. The men were transforming logs floating in the icy water into railroad ties for the Idaho Northern Railway. Suddenly, one of the eight-foot "logs" began to move, and floated unaided toward the depths of Payette Lake.

In 1944, a man named Walter Bowling, who owned a resort at Lake Payette, reported to the *Payette Star News* that he had seen a creature, "a serpent," with several humps resembling a camel's back. That same year, *Time* magazine quoted a Thomas L. Rogers from Boise, saying that at least 30 people

STURGEON
(courtesy of Idaho State Fish and Game Department)

had seen the same creature. He described the head of the creature as resembling a "snub-nosed crocodile."

In 1953, Pauline Miller, a resident of Boise, said she saw a jet-black creature nearly 60 feet long swimming through the Payette Lake waters as she sat looking from an office window at the now-defunct Lake View Lodge.

In 1977, Kathleen Milburn and her son Douglass were fishing off Cougar Island, in the northeast corner of Payette Lake. About 75 yards away, Kathleen suddenly spotted ripples in the water, which she estimated were between 12 and 15 inches high. Within the ripples were three large lumps, which she said looked like three truck innertubes connected. A similar phenomenon was witnessed two weeks later by three patrons eating lunch at the lakeside Log Jam Cafe.

Payette Lake is located in eastern-central Idaho, just north of the town of McCall, some 120 miles north of Boise. The lake is alpine, glacial, cold, and deep — as much as 300 feet in some places. Surrounded by mountains 5000 feet above sea level, it is fed from the north by mountain springs, and drains to the south into the north fork of the Payette River.

For more than 60 years, scores of people have claimed to have seen a creature that the *Payette Star News*, via a reader's contest, named "Sharlie." Witnesses have sworn to lengths of 35, 40, 55, and 60 feet and longer. The colors described include black, silver, brown, and green. Sharlie's head has been likened to that of a crocodile, a fish, a serpent, a cow, and even a bulldog.

There are many who explain Sharlie as a fantasy perpetuated by the local Chamber of Commerce to draw attention and tourism to the area. In a more imaginative and optimistic depiction Sharlie, like Scotland's Loch Ness Monster, is purported to be a prehistoric plesiosaur: trapped in the icy water long ago, it continues to cruise between the lake's surface and bottom, protected from clear identification by the water's inaccessibility. Some have even suggested that Sharlie is merely a line of river otters, swimming in single file in their characteristic undulating manner.

Actually, the most plausible explanation is nearly as fascinating as the legends of sea serpents. The Acipenseridae family of fishes is commonly known as the sturgeons. They are an extremely ancient and primitive species, resembling sharks. The sturgeon's body is covered with thick bony plates, some of which form a row of bony humps along the back, followed by a tall pectoral fin. It forages at the bottom of the body of water, using fleshy feelers about the snout to detect invertebrates, which are sucked into its toothless mouth. Members of the family Acipenseridae are found in oceans, rivers, and lakes throughout the Northern Hemisphere. The family includes the common sturgeon of Scandinavia and the Mediterranean, the beluga (of caviar fame) from the Black Sea in Russia, the lake sturgeon of North America, and the white sturgeon of the Pacific Coast.

Discovered among the sturgeons have been some truly monstrous specimens. Lengths of more than 20 feet and weights of more than 2000 pounds have been claimed for specimens throughout the globe. In Russia, ages for the beluga are claimed to be between 200 and 300 years.

It is altogether possible that subspecies of the sturgeon may survive and thrive in Payette Lake, Idaho. Given the potential for tremendous length, weight, and longevity among the family Acipenseridae, it is easy to imagine that a particularly massive specimen — or even two swimming in close proximity — could give rise to the legend of Sharlie. At a distance, a sturgeon's head may resemble that of a crocodile or a serpent; the row of plates on its back could be the humps so often described by Sharlie witnesses; and its color can appear greenish, brownish, blackish, or silverish, depending on the sky and the cloud cover.

Of course, it is much more fun — and more profitable for the tourist industry of McCall, Idaho — to perpetuate the story of Sharlie the Sea Serpent of Payette Lake. Certainly a landlocked plesiosaur is much more exciting to the general public than a relatively common sturgeon, no matter what the size (never mind that the sturgeon evolved long before the plesiosaur came into existence). But whatever Sharlie is — sturgeon, plesiosaur, or public relations gimmick — it is sure to be a reason to travel to McCall, Idaho, and Payette Lake for years to come.

SOURCES: Accola, John. "Sharlie: Tales of the Lake Monster Resurface." *The Idaho Statesman*, October 16, 1977. / Brown, Jayne. "Sharlie the Serpent of Payette Lakes." *1961 Idaho Fishing and Hunting Guide. /* Rowland, Frank P. *Founding of McCall, Idaho.* Caldwell, Idaho: Caston, 1960. / Williams, Mary Jane. "Sharlie — The Sea Serpent." *Incredible Idaho*, summer 1971.

Illinois

ANIMAL: Morris
DOB: 1961
DOD: 1978
DESCRIPTION: Tiger house cat, orange and white striped coat, 15 pounds.

Hollywood loves its legends of discovery. Lana Turner, discovered in the Top Hat Cafe (Hollywood lore has it as Schwab's Drug Store) in 1936, went

MORRIS
(courtesy of Edelman Public Relations Worldwide)

on to fame as Tinsel Town's Sweater Girl and one of filmdom's most luminous stars. Robert Redford, discovered after taking acting classes in order to jump-start a career as a set designer, went from starving artist to one of the most recognized names in motion picture history.

Morris the Cat was discovered in 1966 at a Humane Society animal shelter in Hinsdale, Illinois, a southwestern suburb of Chicago. Within five years, he would become the most popular, most recognized feline in America.

Animal talent scout and manager Bob Martwick found the large orange-and-white tiger cat in a cage at the crowded shelter. As was typical for springtime in Chicago, strays were being brought in from all over northeast Illinois, and many of them would be destroyed to make room for the strays to follow. The tiger cat was scheduled next — down to eight lives in less than 20 minutes. The tiger cat caught Martwick's eye not only because of his unusual size, but also because he carried himself with a calm dignity amidst the chaos of the shelter. As Martwick took him out of the cage to have a better look at him, the cat attempted neither to flee nor to fight; it nonchalantly stood at Martwick's feet, looking him over just as Martwick was assessing the cat. Placid, even-tempered, and affectionate, he was just the sort of feline Martwick was seeking. Martwick paid the shelter five dollars, and he and the tiger cat left together. Neither life would ever be the same.

The first "9 Lives Presents Morris" commercial was filmed on location in Chicago in May of 1969 and ran for the first time in the city on May 5. The same commercial aired nationally on June 19, 1969. It was an instant hit. Morris immediately became the spokes-animal for 9 Lives cat food, and between 1969 and 1978, he starred in more than 40 commercials for the brand, produced by Leo Burnett Advertising.

While actor John Erwin provided the voice that said, "The cat that doesn't act finicky loses control of the owner," Morris clearly provided the character and the attitude. The storyline for the ads was always the same: An off-camera female voice would offer Morris some 9 Lives cat food. Morris would go into his finicky act, smugly wisecracking at his owner, refusing to show any interest in the food or to lower his facade of disdain. By the time the commercial was over, however, Morris would be face-first in the kitty dish, devouring the meal as if there were no tomorrow. Later versions of the commercial included "Doll Buggy," "Tea Party," "Girl Friend," and "Morris and Albert."

Morris's television spots were so popular that a full-time secretary named Nancy Brady was hired to handle his fan mail. In 1972 Morris was offered a starring role beside Burt Reynolds and Dyan Cannon in the detective thriller *Shamus* (1973). In July 1973, Morris was the recipient of the American Humane Association's twenty-third Annual Patsy Award as the outstanding animal star in America.

Morris's popularity continued through the seventies and into the eighties. Although the original Morris died in 1978 at the age of 19, Morris II stepped into the role, the character's popularity continued. In fact, 9 Lives ran a publicity stunt in August of 1987 announcing that Morris had thrown his hat — or perhaps, flea collar — into the ring to campaign for president of the United States. His platform included the values of "life, liberty, and the pursuit of din-din."

In the final analysis, what was it that made Morris such a charismatic figure? This typical sample from his voluminous fan mail seems to explain:

Dear Morris:
You are my hero. You have liberated the cats of America from the "soft and purry and sleepy little kitten on the best chair" cat.
We love you.

> Sincerely yours,
> Pussy C. Willow

SOURCES: Daniels, Mary. *Morris.* New York: William Morrow, 1974. / "Morris Tosses His Flea Collar into the Ring." *Chicago Tribune,* August 19, 1987. Sec. 1, p. 4.

Indiana

ANIMAL: Dan Patch
DOB: April 29, 1896
DOD: July 11, 1916
DESCRIPTION: American Standardbred horse (*Equus caballus*), mahogany-colored coat.

Among the best known theatrical productions of the last 50 years is Meredith Willson's *The Music Man,* the 1958 play about a conman who swindles the turn-of-the-century town of River City, Iowa. In the memorable musical number "Trouble," Harold Hill stirs the God-fearing souls of River City by foretelling the coming of great evils due to the idle minds of the town's youth. Among the evils is a new style of horse racing in which the rider actually sits on the horse. Hill shocks his listeners with his suggestion of a jockey "sitting on Dan Patch." The reference likely escaped the ear of most listeners, but the lyric still reminds one of the genteel side of the sport of kings — harness racing. In the fledgling years of this century, Dan Patch, from Oxford, Indiana, was the greatest harness racehorse of all.

No jockey ever sat on Dan Patch, who pulled the sulky — the two-wheel, single-rider carriage of harness racing — better than any horse before him, and most after him. Between 1903 and 1910, Dan Patch broke the world's record for harness racing 14 times. He was the only world champion who never lost a race, and the only pacer to break his own and the world's record four consecutive years. At the Minnesota State Fair in 1906, he broke the world record of 1:55 for the mile, and he went on to break the two-minute mile barrier on 35 separate occasions.

This success lifted Dan Patch to a celebrity status few horses — indeed, few athletes of any kind — have ever enjoyed. He traveled the Midwest in his own specially designed railroad car. Thousands of fans lined up to view this horse, to touch him, to simply be in his presence. Said one observer, "Men, women, and children seemed content just to see him — as if he were George Washington or Abraham Lincoln."

DAN PATCH
(courtesy of Minnesota Historical Society)

Appearing at county fairs and race tracks, he was greeted by souvenir hunters and brass bands. So frenzied were his receptions that his owner worried about the harm that might befall the horse at the hands of his fans. But Dan Patch was reportedly unfazed by the attention, and at times seemed almost to relish it. His kindly manner toward the human world no doubt reflected the luxurious treatment he received from his owners.

When Dan Patch was born on April 29, 1896, harness racing had been in existence in America for more than 200 years. Dan Patch was born to a mare named Zelica on a farm in Oxford, Indiana. His owner, Dan Messner, apparently felt that the scraggly, awkward colt would amount to nothing. The colt was named Dan after Messner, and Patch after his sire, Joe Patchen.

Dan paced his first race at the Benton County Fair in Boswell, Indiana, on August 30, 1900. He toured other race tracks in the Great Lakes Region for a couple of years, until tragedy struck in 1901.

Dan Patch's sister and stable mate was named Lady Patch. One night, someone entered the stable where the pair was bedded and poisoned Lady Patch. Convinced that the poison had been meant for Dan Patch, Messner quickly sold him to a horse broker named C.F. Sturgis for $20,000, then the largest sum ever paid for a pacer. In December of 1903 Sturgis sold Dan Patch for $60,000 to Marion Willis Savage of Minneapolis, who remained Dan Patch's owner through his heyday.

Savage and Dan Patch were virtually inseparable for the rest of their lives. The two remained at the top of their sport until Dan Patch retired, and on top of the world until the end. Savage grew rich as Dan Patch grew famous. It was once estimated that Dan Patch's earnings for Savage and himself well exceeded three million dollars. During the first decade of the twentieth century, his name could be found on cigars, chewing tobacco, hobby horses, wagons, sleds, washing machines, and pillows. Even a dance step, called the Dan Patch two-step, was named in his honor.

As the records fell one by one, the throngs poured out to watch the king of harness racing. More than 600,000 came out to see him during his marvelous career. Finally, Dan Patch went to stud on Savage's farm near Minneapolis, Minnesota, in 1910. There he continued to draw adoring visitors.

On July 4, 1916, both Dan Patch and M.W. Savage became ill. Dan Patch died on July 11 at the age of 20. Grief stricken and in shock, Savage died the next day. Funerals for the horse and his owner were held at the same hour.

The nation mourned. A cartoon in one local newspaper depicted Dan Patch surrounded by a winner's wreath. The caption beneath read simply, "The King is Dead."

SOURCES: Cline, Pat. "Dan Patch Raced Here." *Montgomery*, 1977. P. 16. / Macy, Roscoe. "Million-Dollar Show-Off." *Esquire*, 1947. / Pines, Philip A. *The Complete Book of Harness Racing*. New York: Grosset & Dunlop, 1970. Pp. 41–46.

ANIMAL: Old Ben
DOB: January 1902
DOD: February 1910
DESCRIPTION: Heresford-shorthorn steer, reddish-brown hide, corkscrew
  left horn; 16', 2" long, 4720 pounds.

This story is a lot of bull. It also happens to be true!

In January of 1902, on a farm in Miami, Indiana (just north of Kokomo), a crossbred Hereford calf named Ben was born. Ben weighed 125 pounds at birth. Given that the average weight of a newborn calf is 50 to 100 pounds, this birth was not such an important event. The calf was certainly large, but not remarkably so. At least, not yet.

Soon, however, Ben began to grow—at an incredible rate. Raised by Mike and John Murphy on a cattle farm in Miami, Ben weighed 1800 pounds at 18 months. By 1906, at the age of four, he weighed more than 4000 pounds. At his maximum size, he stood 6' 4" tall at the forequarter, had a girth of 13' 8", and measured between 16' 2" and 16' 8" long, depending on which source one consults. This size compares roughly to that of the average mini-van. Ben's weight peaked at 4720 pounds which, according to Guinness, made him the heaviest steer in history — the history of Indiana, of the United States, of the world.

The Hereford breed has been popular as a beef cattle for more than 150 years in the United States. The breed was originally brought from Hereford County in England to the United States. Henry Clay brought the breed over for his farm in Kentucky in 1837, but it wasn't until 1850 that Herefords were imported by farmers and ranchers in large quantities. Herefords became popular because they are heartier, require less care, and can survive the elements better than most breeds. Because Old Ben was not pure Hereford, but rather a crossbreed between Hereford and Shorthorn, he was never actually registered by the Murphys.

Once word of this huge steer spread, Old Ben became an instant celebrity. He was exhibited by the Murphys at circuses, fairs, and sideshows. He won numerous ribbons and awards, not only for his immense size, but for his handsome appearance and fine lines. His hide was mostly reddish-brown except for his feet and lower legs. And while his right horn grew straight and normal, his left horn twisted in corkscrew, giving the steer an even more distinctive appearance — as if he needed it.

Old Ben's celebrated life came to an end in the winter of 1910. He was destroyed after slipping on some ice and breaking a leg. At the time he still weighed his peak 4720 pounds. Old Ben's hide was saved and preserved by taxidermy, mounted within a special enclosure at Highland Park in southwest Kokomo. Undoubtedly, the Murphys wanted to be sure Old Ben was preserved for posterity. Otherwise, how could future generations believe so much bull?

SOURCES: Cavinder, Fred D. *The Indiana Book of Records, Firsts, and Fascinating Facts.* Bloomington: Indiana University Press, 1985. / Wood, Gerald L. *Animal Facts and Feats: A Guinness Record of the Animal Kingdom.* Garden City, N.Y.: Doubleday, 1972.

Iowa

ANIMAL: General J. Pershing
DOB: 1915 (approximately)
DOD: 1918
DESCRIPTION: Old English rooster, black torso and wings, approximately 12" tall.

When former United States Patent Office clerk Clara Barton (1821–1912) founded the American National Red Cross in 1881, she no doubt expected many things from this foundation. She expected it to aid the sick, wounded, and

GENERAL J. PERSHING
(courtesy of Exira Public Library, Exira, Iowa)

imprisoned, and the families of the dead, during wartime. She also expected the Red Cross to care for the survivors of famines, floods, earthquakes, and cyclones throughout the United States. She also expected to have to rely on the generosity of people to provide for the foundation to do its work. But Barton, also known as the "Angel of the Battlefield," could not have expected that she would ever have a benefactor quite like General Jack Pershing. For General Pershing was a rooster.

In 1917, with the entrance of the United States into World War I, the Red Cross suddenly found itself overwhelmed with duties both home and abroad, with not nearly enough funds to support them all.

While soldiers fought the war in France, citizens on the home front did whatever they could to raise funds for the Red Cross, which had traveled to France with the soldiers. Many communities began holding benefit sales in which items donated by individuals were auctioned off, with the proceeds going directly to the Red Cross. On December 15, 1917, a benefit sale was held in the town of Fontanelle, Iowa, about 60 miles southwest of Des Moines. Among the items donated for the sale was a big black Old English rooster, contributed by naturalized German farmhand Mark Dunkerton, who eventually sent two sons to serve in the war. Under the direction of professional auctioneer Col. D.R. Jones, the rooster was sold for 50 cents. However, the man who bought it decided he didn't want it; he merely wanted to donate the money to the cause. So back onto the auction block went the rooster, and again it was sold for 50 cents. The second buyer, like the first, returned the rooster to the auctioneer.

The pattern was repeated several times. The custom developed that each buyer would keep possession of the black rooster for no more than five minutes. Then the rooster would return to the auctioneer, who would begin the bidding anew. By the end of the evening's proceedings, the rooster had raised $292.00, all of which went to the Fontanelle chapter of the Red Cross. "For the benefit of the boys over there" became a rallying cry for the buyers. It was at this benefit sale that the rooster was christened "General Jack Pershing."

At the end of the sale, auctioneer Jones took General Pershing home, since none of the buyers would take him. He fashioned a coop for the general and took him in as his own pet. The rooster became quite tame, and Jones decided to take him to all of the sales over which he was asked to preside.

Jones brought General Jack Pershing to Red Cross benefit sales throughout Iowa and South Dakota. So successful were these sales that Jones retired from his other duties to devote all his time and energy to raising money for the Red Cross.

With General Pershing sitting on his shoulder, Jones would open the auction with an impassioned plea: "Listen, folks," he would say, "Jack and I are here to raise money for the Red Cross." Jones would go on to explain to his listeners how their money could do so much for the "boys over there," and for the Red Cross, which offered care and comfort for the soldiers. The crowds would open their hearts and their wallets and readily participate in the repeated selling of Jack Pershing. The rooster was lively and played to the crowd, and it would crow and "cock-a-doodle-doo!" as the crowd cheered. Jones and Jack Pershing attended more than 35 different sales in six months, and Jones sold the rooster more than 9000 times in one year for the benefit of the Red Cross.

The largest auction involving D.A. Jones and General Jack Pershing took place on January 19, 1918, in Exira, Iowa, 59 miles west of Des Moines. That day Pershing was bought again and again for total of $7,316.50. This was the highest amount raised at one auction involving the black rooster. A small village of 168 people in South Dakota managed to raise $5040, the second highest amount raised. In all, General Jack Pershing, in a space of 12 months, raised more than $40,000 for the American Red Cross through benefit sales.

General Jack Pershing lived the remainder of his years in Jones's own private poultry flock in Exira, Iowa. As the rooster grew older, Jones decided to have him preserved while he still appeared strong and healthy. He commended him to the care of taxidermist E.C. Wilson, who quietly put General Jack Pershing to rest.

With funds collected from local residents, General Jack Pershing was mounted and presented for posterity to the State Historical Building in Des Moines. In a glass case in the World War I Exhibit Room, he stands evermore, reminding the citizens of Iowa of the nobility of the cause of the American Red Cross, and the generosity of the people who gave to it.

SOURCE: "What Has Happened to Them?" *Des Moines Tribune*, January 1, 1962. P. 7.

Kansas

ANIMAL: Comanche
DOB: 1860
DOD: November 7, 1891
DESCRIPTION: Saddle horse (*Equus caballus*), bay coat, 15.5 hands high, 940 pounds.

Captain Frederick Benteen's small party from the seventh Cavalry set out on the afternoon of June 27, 1876. The men on horseback rode nervously toward Little Bighorn River and the valley that surrounded it. As they crossed the summit of the little hill, calamity lay before them. Everywhere, as far as the eye could see, bodies of fallen United States Cavalry soldiers lay in pools of blood. More than 200 men, the entirety of four troops led by General George A. Custer, had been destroyed by the Sioux warriors of Crazy Horse and Sitting Bull.

Suddenly, a slight trace of movement could be detected off in the distance. As they approached, the soldiers found a large brown horse standing alone in a flat near the Indian village, like a sentinel at some military graveyard. Seven bullets had pierced the flesh of the steed: one through the neck, one just behind the front shoulder (passing through the lungs), and one through the hindquarters, with the rest apparently having nicked the flesh at various points. This was the mount of Captain Myles Keogh, a subordinate commander under General Custer. (It was later discovered that one of Keogh's legs had been broken by the same bullet that had penetrated behind the horse's front shoulder.) The mount's name was Comanche. How the horse had managed to remain standing was beyond imagination.

Many theories have attempted to explain exactly what happened in Southern Montana on June 25, 1876. Historians have pointed out that the battle would not have occurred had white men, greedy for gold and confident in the idea of "manifest destiny," not trespassed on the Sioux territory, and sought to push the natives off their land. This was just another example of the betrayal

COMANCHE
(courtesy of David McKinney, University of Kansas)

and deception played out by the Europeans, and the massacre of Custer and his men was the last desperate stand by the Sioux to protect their land and their culture.

Of the battle itself, some have said that Custer ignored warnings that 2000 to 4000 Sioux waited for his 250 soldiers. Others have said that had he brought just one Rodman gun or one Gatling gun with him, the battle's outcome would have been substantially reversed. Still others have accused Custer of seeking gold in the area himself, citing his personal avarice as the motivation for his foolish campaign. Whether due to greed, arrogance, incompetence, or — as some have suggested — derangement, one thing is for sure: The battle was a disaster for the Seventh Cavalry. And Comanche was the last living thing on the battlefield from Custer's side.

Badly wounded, the horse had not been captured by Sioux, as was the custom for healthy horses. Comanche was brought back to Fort Riley, Kansas, 63 miles west of Topeka, where the seventh Cavalry was stationed. Through the winter of 1876-77, Comanche was nursed back to health by a Lieutenant Godfrey of the seventh Cavalry, and by a blacksmith. Following the return of Comanche's health, Colonel Samuel D. Sturgis issued a special set of orders regarding the care and comfort of the animal, stating

His kind treatment and comfort should be a matter of special pride and solicitude of the Seventh Cavalry, to the end that his life be prolonged to the utmost limit. Wounded and scarred as he is, his very existence speaks in terms more eloquent than words of the desperate struggle against overwhelming numbers; of the hopeless conflict; and of the heroic manner in which all went down on that fatal day....

Among the details of Sturgis's orders were that Comanche would be provided a special stall; would never be ridden under any circumstance; would never be pressed into work of any kind; and would be saddled, bridled, draped in mourning, and led by a mounted trooper at all occasions of ceremony, in memory of the soldiers who died tragically at Little Bighorn. Comanche's life was transformed to one of utmost luxury — for a horse, at least. He made several parade appearances, outfitted as Sturgis had ordered, and continued to live in his special stall.

On November 7, 1891, at the ripe age of 31, Comanche died. The remains were presented to Professor Lewis Lindsay Dyche of the University of Kansas, at the taxidermy laboratory. Dr. Dyche set about preserving and mounting the remains, and when he was done, the story goes, he sent a bill for $400 to the Seventh Cavalry for his services. With the bill was a note, informing the Cavalry that they could forego the invoice if they would allow him to keep Comanche at the museum at the university. The Seventh Cavalry agreed, and Comanche has been there ever since.

After all these years, Comanche remains a focal point of interest for thousands of visitors to the Dyche Museum at the University of Kansas. The viewers come to study the symbol of the struggle between native and immigrant people; the link in the transformation of wilderness to civilization; and the remains of the last living being at the Battle of Little Bighorn.

SOURCES: Davis, Kenneth C. *Don't Know Much About History*. New York: Avon, 1990. Pp. 193–195. / Graham, William Alexander. *The Custer Myth*. New York: Bonanza 1953. Pp. 247–250. / *Indian Depredations, Battles and Treaties*. Lawrence Journal-World, vol. 3, Jan 13, 1932.

Kentucky

ANIMAL: Man o' War
DOB: March 29, 1917
DOD: November 1, 1947
DESCRIPTION: Thoroughbred horse (*Equus caballus*), large, muscular form, deep chestnut-red coat.

Man o' War was a thoroughbred heralded as much for his accomplishments in the pasture as for those on the race track. Not only was "Big Red" successful in competition, but his lineage produced several colts who grew up to be champions as well.

Man o' War was born on March 29, 1917, at Nursery Stud, Kentucky, and raised at Faraway Farms outside of Paris, Kentucky. "Big Red," as he was known for his tremendous size and stride and his beautiful chestnut coloring, was owned by Samuel D. Riddle. Riddle had bought Man o' War from Major August Belmont in 1918 for $5000. Over the years, Big Red would net more than $240,000 for him.

Between 1919 and 1920, Man o' War won 20 of 21 races, including the Preakness and the Belmont Stakes. He failed to win the Triple Crown, however, because Riddle felt that April was far too early in the season for a three-year-old to race at the Kentucky Derby. During his brief career, Man o' War set five records in distances of one mile to one mile and five-eighths; by the time of his retirement, he had set 11 records in all, many that lasted past his lifetime. In 1950, a poll taken among Associated Press writers named Man o' War the greatest racehorse of the first half of the twentieth century.

During his career, Man o' War was defeated by only one horse: Upset, at Saratoga on August 13, 1919. Due to a mix-up at the starting barrier (something for which Man o' War was well known, due to his overanxiousness at the start of races), Man o' War started in the wrong direction, and it took him half a mile to catch up to the rest of the field. Still, he lost by only half a length.

Man o' War was put to stud at age four, and he sired 64 stakes horses. Among his most successful offspring were the following:

> War Admiral, Man o' War's greatest son, who won the Triple Crown in 1937, one of only nine horses to do so. By then, apparently, Riddle had reversed his rule about three-year-olds racing in April.
> Battleship, who in 1938 became the first American horse to win the Grand National Steeplechase in England. Battleship, because of his small stature, became known as the "American Pony."
> Clyde Van Drusen, a gelding, who won the Kentucky Derby in 1929.

In all, Man o' War sired 379 foals who, among them, won more than 1200 races. His greatest characteristics of speed, stature, and endurance were passed on through his lineage, even through less than top-quality mares. An incredible 80 percent of Man o' War's offspring raced at the track.

Even though his actual racing career was less than two years, racing fans everywhere came to worship him as the greatest champion of all. During his 20-year career as stud, more than one million visitors made the pilgrimage — and for many, that's exactly what it was — to Faraway Farms. There they could gaze in wonder at that big red horse.

In 1947, after having outlived most of the champion foals he had sired, Man o' War died at the age of 30. More than 2000 horse lovers attended the funeral rites at Faraway Farms.

SOURCES: Chew, Peter. *The Kentucky Derby: The First 100 Years*. Boston: Houghton Mifflin, 1974. Pp. 4, 6, 8–9, 14, 24. / Wilding, Suzanne, and Del Baldo, Anthony. *The Triple Crown Winners: The Story of America's Nine Superstar Race Horses*. New York: Parents' Magazine Press, 1975.

Louisiana

ANIMAL: Mike
DOB: 1935
DOD: June 29, 1956
DESCRIPTION: Bengal tiger (*Panthera tigris*), burnt orange coat with black stripes, approximately 9' long, 400 to 500 pounds.

In June of 1863, in the epic Civil War battle at Gettysburg, there was a brigade of soldiers from Louisiana led by Captain Harry Hays. During one stage of the battle, a stronghold of Union artillery led by Captain R. Bruce Ricketts was perched on Cemetery Ridge, intent on holding the ridge, preventing Confederate soldiers from advancing upward. Hays' brigade charged up Cemetery Ridge anyway, quickly subduing Ricketts' battery and quieting the pounding from its guns.

The brigade from Louisiana possessed a fighting ferocity scarcely equaled by any other on either side of the war. This unit of soldiers became aptly known as the "Louisiana Tigers." There were many LSU cadets among the Tigers, including Major David French Boyd, who would later become president of Louisiana State University. After the Civil War, in memory of the Louisiana Tigers, the tiger was adopted as the symbol for the university.

In 1936, LSU students developed a fund to purchase a mascot. With the $750 collected, a one-year-old tiger named "Sheik" was purchased from the Little Rock Zoo in Arkansas. The tiger was renamed "Mike," and appeared on campus for the first time on October 21, 1936.

From that day forward, Mike was "the sheik" on campus. He followed the football team to colleges around the country, appearing at every game, both home and away. Visitors from other states would pay homage to the regal feline, who seemed to take it all in with a calm befitting the true king of beasts. On campus, he lived in a specially constructed lair, called the Tiger's Cage, located between what is now Pete Maravich Assembly Center and Tiger Stadium.

The tiger is the largest member of the order Felus. Native to Asia, it is a solitary, immensely skilled hunter, able to kill animals several times its own weight. In its marvelously beautiful (and unfortunately for the tiger, very valuable) coat, the tiger stalks its prey with almost invisible stealth. It can cover 40 feet in

MIKE THE TIGER
(courtesy of LSU Office of Public Relations)

a single leap, and brings down its prey with a mercifully quick combination of fang and claw. It may be the most efficient land predator in the world, and observers say that no words can adequately depict the sight of an adult tiger in the wild.

Mike the tiger died on June 29, 1956. He was 21 years old, quite a long life for a tiger; some claim it as a record for longevity among captive tigers. Immediately, letters poured into the university campus, expressing the regret of thousands of LSU alumni from around the world at the death of their beloved mascot. Some of the letters recalled seeing Mike at football games; others described visiting Mike on campus. Many equated the passing of Mike to the passing of a family member, and one letter, from a Mrs. A.H. Beaudry, told of a stuffed "Mike the tiger," that was presented to her son Dick as a boy. The stuffed Mike apparently accompanied Dick through his childhood and a great portion of his adult life as well.

More than $2500 was quickly donated for the purpose of having Mike the tiger stuffed and mounted. He now resides in a glass case in the Museum of Natural Science at Foster Hall, where visitors still come to see him.

> The Reaper favors no beast or man
> And so your cage becomes an empty cell;
> But Mike you had another home as well
> Within the heart of every loyal fan…
> And each new team shall help exemplify
> A Tiger Spirit that shall never die.
> — The Bengal Bard — O. Hupperdick

SOURCES: "In Memory of Mike." *LSU Alumni News*, September/October 1956. / Scott, Jack Denton. "The Fiery Tiger." *Marvels and Mysteries of Our Animal World*. Pleasantville, N.Y.: Reader's Digest Association, 1964. Pp. 117–120.

Maine

ANIMAL: Andre
DOB: 1961
DOD: 1986
DESCRIPTION: Atlantic harbor seal (*Phoca vitulina*), spotted gray coat, 6' long, 240 pounds.

It is rare that a pinniped is pitted against a state governor in a contest of political will. But just such a conflict arose in 1979 in Maine between Governor Joseph Brennen and a seal called Andre. In an extremely ill-conceived statement, Brennen criticized the press of Maine for spending too much time and coverage on Andre the seal (who by then had been lifted to the status of local legend in the central coast town of Rockport) and not enough time on "more important" issues. So outraged was the local citizenry by Brennen's remarks that dozens of protest letters poured in from the voters, and the governor was forced to release a conciliatory statement to the press.

Such was the life and political clout of Andre the seal, certainly the most unusual and celebrated seal in American history. Not only did Andre manage to bridge the gulf between a wild and a domesticated existence, but he did it in a way that brought excitement and notoriety in nearly every adventure he had.

In the wild, the harbor seal (*Phoca vitulina*) can grow to a length of eight feet, and a weight of more than 300 pounds. It is common on both coasts of the United States, where it spends much of its time swimming, feeding, or "hauling out" onto rocky shores to sun itself. Its blubbery hide can be any color from beige to spotted to gray. Historically the hide has been of no commercial value, but the harbor seal has been harassed for generations, generally

AN ANDRE FACSIMILE
(courtesy of Ken Bach, Marine Mammal Center, Marin County, CA)

by fishermen who regard it as competition for their catches. If they can avoid predators and disease, a harbor seal can live more than 25 years. Andre's life in the wild would have been painful, however, if not for the good heart of a resident of Rockport, Maine.

In 1961, Harry Goodridge, an arborist (tree surgeon) and scuba diver, found a two-day-old harbor seal pup by itself on a haul-out point in Penobscot Bay, Maine, called Robinson Rock. Apparently abandoned by its mother, the seal would have been doomed to slow starvation or shark attack had it been left to itself.

Over the next four years Goodridge suckled Andre on a sponge-rubber mother substitute, and weaned him on fish. Andre would take up residence in the house of Toots the dog; he'd swim with Harry in his scuba gear; he'd go on trips with Harry and family in the car. Harry taught him to perform tricks: shooting basketballs through hoops, blowing horns, jumping through hoops. Andre developed all the behaviors of a trained circus seal. All the time, Andre remained a free, wild seal. Every day Harry would take him down to the harbor near his house in Rockport and set him free. "If he departed for good, that was fine with me." Even the fisherman grew fond of him, and they kept a look out for him as he traversed the coast of Maine. A harbor pen was constructed for Andre to use, but Goodridge would free him from it on a regular basis, especially each winter, when he could swim to a warmer sea. This was perhaps the first time a wild creature learned tricks in a free-release situation: that is, a set-up in which Andre could leave anytime he decided to.

In 1962 Andre began wandering down the coast of Maine, especially in winter. But he always returned to Rockport and Harry Goodridge. He became a local celebrity for his wanderings and performances, and was elected honorary harbor master of Rockport in 1964. In 1967, Andre was filmed by Charles Kuralt and CBS, and his fame spread far beyond the coast of Maine.

As Andre grew older, winters became especially hard on him, and he would often return to Rockport battered and bruised from his travels — many times from fights with other bull harbor seals. So, in 1973, Harry decided to loan Andre to Boston's New England Aquarium each winter. Each spring, Andre would be turned loose from the aquarium and would swim straight up the coast to Rockport Harbor again. The newspapers chronicled his yearly sojourns, and fan mail came to Andre from around the world.

In July of 1975, Goodridge was visited by officials from the National Marine Fisheries Service (NMFS), who claimed that his pen might be in violation of the Marine Mammal Protection Act. The officials threatened to confiscate the pen. Soon the press got wind of the visit from the NMFS. The *Portland Press Herald*'s headline read, "Andre Seal in Big Trouble with Feds." Civic leaders began urging the NMFS officials to let Andre be, and letters started pouring into the NMFS office, many describing the officials in particularly nasty ways. Even Congressman Peter Kyros, Senator Ed Muskie, and Senator Bill Hathaway stepped into the fray. By the end of the summer, the NMFS officials made a sheepish about-face, and Andre and Harry were allowed to keep their pen.

By 1977, at the age of 16, Andre found his luck turning a bit sour. He bit an Albion man in a mishap with his rowboat, and police confined Andre to his pen. This episode was quickly forgotten, however, and a statue of Andre was erected in Rockport's Marine Park in 1978. By 1981, Andre was wintering at Mystic Marinelife Aquarium in Connecticut. In 1985, 24 years old and nearly blind, Andre made his last coastal swim to Maine. A few weeks later, Andre was found dead outside of Rockland, Maine, south of Rockport. He was the apparent loser in a fight with another seal. A brief funeral was convened for perhaps the world's most famous wild harbor seal.

But even after his death, Andre continued to draw notice and inspire controversy. In 1994, Paramount released the film *Andre*, based on Harry Goodridge's book *A Seal Called Andre*. Much to the chagrin of Goodrich and marine biologists around the country, the filmmakers cast a California sea lion to play the part of Andre the harbor seal. So obvious are the differences between harbor seals (phocids) and sea lions (otariids) that, as one former trainer who worked with Andre at the New England Aquarium said, "It's like doing 'Born Free' with a bear."

The film was less than well received at the box office. Yet Andre himself— through Harry Goodridge's book and the statue that stands at Rockport Harbor — remains a happy memory to the people of Maine, and to all who enjoy the idea of free and harmonious co-existence between humans and marine mammals.

SOURCES: Dietz, Lew, and Goodridge, Harry. *A Seal Called Andre*. New York, Praeger, 1975. / Routhier, Ray. "For Andre the Movie, Hollywood's Approval of Seal." *Maine Sunday Telegram*, July 31, 1994.

Maryland

ANIMAL: Mary Ann
DOB: Probably around 1920
DOD: March 1941
DESCRIPTION: Asiatic elephant (*Elephas maximus*), approximately 84 " tall, 6,000 pounds

Officials at the zoo at Druid Hill Park should have known from the first day that Mary Ann was going to be a handful. It was Easter Sunday morning in 1925. Children from Baltimore and all throughout Maryland, whose nickels and dimes had been collected through a newspaper campaign to help pay for Mary Ann to be brought to the zoo, lined the streets between Bay Shore and Druid Hill Park. Baltimore's mayor, Howard Jackson, with a collection of the city's VIPs, a brass band, and hundreds of happy Baltimore residents, awaited Mary Ann's arrival at the park entrance. Mary Ann, the zoo's first elephant, would be transported via flatbed truck to her enclosure. However, as it happened, that trip would not be completed until late Easter Sunday afternoon.

It quickly became apparent to the city of Baltimore that this elephant was full of mischief. For seven long and arduous hours, Mary Ann refused to board the flatbed truck at the train station. Fifteen men, an animal trainer, and a circus manager employed a number of methods to coax the three-ton pachyderm onto the truck. They tried pushing and pulling her, but she would not budge. They tried to tempt her with fruits, oats, even an onion, but she would not be lured. When they tried to fool her onto the gangplank, she dug her heels deeper into the earth. When the crane was wheeled in, she would not hold still long enough for the harness to be attached. When they tried blindfolding her, she threatened to lie down.

Then, whether because she was bored or irritated or because she had simply concluded she could easily win this contest of wills, Mary Ann ended the dispute. At 3:14 P.M., she was aboard the flatbed, headed for the zoo. At 5:24 P.M., she entered Druid Hill Park Zoo.

Throughout her 16-year residence at the zoo, the elephant did nothing to abate the reputation that eventually won her the title of "Mischievous Mary Ann." She was known to reach her prehensile trunk through the bars of her cage and swoop bicycles out from underneath the rear ends of children. Zoo patrons unwary enough to stick their umbrellas or canes into the elephant enclosure soon found their belongings confiscated by her. One story tells of how she ripped a sweater right off the back of a little girl and ate it like a bale of hay. Even the ice man, on a delivery to her cage, lost his hat to Mischievous Mary Ann. Despite her pranks — or perhaps because of them — Mary Ann became the star attraction for Druid Hill Park. Her fiendish behavior made Baltimore legend, and children and adults alike would swarm around her cage, waiting wide-eyed to see what kind of stunt she would pull off next.

The size, strength, appetite, and longevity of elephants are legendary. But their hearing is equally phenomenal. Their huge ears easily take in sounds from their native habitats that human beings would have a hard time detecting. They use this sensitivity to sound in their communication, emitting low-frequency sounds over their vast ranges. Their hearing also serves to quickly warn them of the approach of predators — should there be any brave or foolish enough to attempt an attack. It is this skill at auditory detection, however, that may have led to Mary Ann's demise.

In 1940, the zoo began construction of a new polar bear habitat next to the elephant enclosure. The pounding of the construction was painful to Mary Ann's sensitive ears, and it disturbed both her behavior and her sleep. She would refuse to lie down, obtaining whatever sleep she could in an upright position. Of course, she got little rest, and her health began to deteriorate. Finally, one March night in 1941, Mary Ann collapsed from exhaustion. Falling down, she sprained her back, and died soon afterwards. The zoo officials took her out on the same flatbed truck on which she had arrived on Easter Sunday in 1925. But now it was to the tears — instead of the cheers — of the children of Baltimore.

Mischievous Mary Ann was buried at Rosa Bonheur Memorial Park in Baltimore.

SOURCES: "Mary Ann Safely Housed after Triumphant Ride to Druid Hill Zoo." *Baltimore Sun*, April 14, 1925. / Sandler, Gilbert. "Baltimore Glimpses: Mischievous Mary Ann." *Baltimore Evening Sun*, n.d.

Massachusetts

ANIMAL: Paul Revere's horse
DOB: Unknown
DOD: Unknown
DESCRIPTION: Narragansett Pacer (*Equus caballus*), sorrel or orange-brown coat, 13–14 hands high.

> So through the night rode Paul Revere;
> And through the night went his cry of alarm

> To every Middlesex village and farm,
> —A cry of defiance and not of fear,
> A voice in the darkness, a knock on the door
> And a word that shall echo forevermore!
> For, borne on the night-wind of the Past,
> Through all our history, through the last,
> In the hour or darkness and peril and need,
> The people will waken and listen to hear
> The hurrying hoof-beats of that steed,
> And the midnight Message of Paul Revere.
> —"Paul Revere's Ride," Henry Wadsworth Longfellow

Is there an American schoolchild (former or current) who has never heard the words of this famous poem, or has no mental image of this famous ride? Paragraphs and pages, articles and books have been written to describe and analyze and mythologize this icon of the American Revolution. And of course, plenty of details have been gathered about the most famous herald in American history:

* He was a son of French Huguenots, born in Boston in 1735.

* He was a silversmith, like his father, learning his trade in an apprenticeship with a John Coney in Boston. His most famous creation was engraving and printing of the March 1770 Boston Massacre. He was also a maker of false teeth.

* Revere was an equestrian from childhood; he rode merely for pleasure, since he needed no horse for his smithery. He owned a horse — which he probably used for carriage rides, or for duck-hunting outside Boston — but it was not the horse upon which he made his legendary ride.

* He was a "Son of Liberty" alongside rabble-rouser Samuel Adams, chief architect of the Boston Tea Party, and John Hancock, chief financier of the Boston rebellion.

* His participation during the war itself was largely unnoticed; he served occasionally as a courier for the colonial forces.

* He died on Sunday, May 10, 1818, at the age of 83.

But what of the horse? Who was the steed of "the hurrying hoof-beats"? Wrote Esther Forbes in her work *Paul Revere and the World He Lived In*:

> Now, for the remainder of the night Revere's success, his life and perhaps the life of others, would depend upon this horse. He would adjust the stirrups carefully to his own length, test with a forefinger the snugness of the girths. They must be tight, but not binding. The bit must hang exactly right. In that unhurried moment before mounting, he would measure the courage and stamina of his companion, catch the flash of white in the wild, soft eye, note the impatient stamp of the small hooves, feel under his hand the swelling of muscle along the neck, the strength in withers and loin, his touch and voice assuring the sensitive animal that he was a friend....

The horse was borrowed from Deacon John, son of Samuel Larkin (1701-1784), who owned a livery and many fine horses in the town of Charlestown, just across the Charles River from Boston. The breed was likely a Narragansett Pacer. This was not a large horse — not more than 14 hands high — and it might have been classified as a pony today. And though artists have depicted Revere's horse in a variety of hues, it was probably a sorrel, of brownish-orange coat. This was no Thoroughbred, but probably the typical New England horse, accustomed to transporting its rider in an efficient, sure-footed manner. As to the horse's name, history seems to have no idea.

Revere set up signals with sexton Robert Newman at Christ Church in Boston: One lantern if by land, two if by the Charles River. Late at night on April 18, 1775, Revere spied two lanterns, meaning General Thomas Gage would cross the Charles River from Boston to advance northwest towards a rebel arsenal in Concord. Both Revere and cordwainer Billy Dawes left on separate routes, both headed for Concord, some 18 miles to the northwest.

Charlestown, where Paul Revere began his ride, is now the district of Somersville in modern Boston, 12 miles to the southeast of Lexington. Dawes left first, taking a northern route that was four miles longer. It was after 11:00 P.M. when Paul Revere left, and the moon glowed brightly above him. The horse galloped along the Mystic River and over a plank bridge into Medford. There Revere awoke the captain of the minutemen, and shouted warnings to nearly every home in the village that the British troops were approaching. The minutemen were colonists who for months had been drilling with their mus-kets, preparing for battle. They were ready — at a minute's notice — to repel the British invasion. Church bells rang out, men shouted and grabbed their muskets and powder; women and children found shelter outside town, while riders galloped off in other directions to carry the warning still farther. All along the way, Revere warned of the coming of the British troops under General Thomas Gage. The British were advancing to seize a colonial arsenal in Con-cord, Massachusetts. Revere crossed the Mystic again and raised the warning through Menotomy (modern-day Arlington). He arrived in Lexington at about midnight. He warned rebel leaders John Hancock and Samuel Adams, and the minutemen prepared for the British approach. As the minutemen of Lexing-ton took their positions, Dawes and Revere headed toward Concord, Massa-chusetts, another six miles up the path. Outside Lexington they were joined by a patriotic doctor from Concord named Samuel Prescott. The three men were soon stopped by a six-man British patrol, guns drawn and pointed. Dawes and Revere were arrested by the British, but Prescott managed to jump his horse over a stone wall and escape, racing all the way to Concord to warn the minutemen there. The officers forced Revere from his horse, and one of them confiscated it, claiming it as its own. That was the last Revere ever saw of the "Good Larkin Horse," which from then on was probably used by the British Army.

Meanwhile, in Lexington, 77 ragtag minutemen engaged the advancing 700-strong British army on a field of grass. From somewhere a shot rang out;

the British broke ranks, and suddenly gunfire from both sides volleyed across the green. Within moments, eight minutemen lay dead on the Lexington Green. This was the "shot heard 'round the world"; this was the beginning of the American Revolution.

SOURCES: Forbes, Esther. *Paul Revere and the World He Lived In*. Boston: Houghton Mifflin, 1942. / Longfellow, Henry Wadsworth. "Paul Revere's Ride."

Michigan

ANIMAL: Peter the Great
DOB: 1895
DOD: 1923
DESCRIPTION: American Standardbred horse (*Equus caballus*), approximately 16 hands high, dark brown coat.

On the campus of Western Michigan University stands a monument to the Standardbred trotting horse Peter the Great. The monument is located on land once owned by railroad contractor Daniel D. Streeter, who owned Peter the Great until 1898. Streeter lived in the house that has served as the home of the president of WMU. Though the monument commemorates Peter the Great's world-record mile run in 1898 at the Kentucky Futurity, it is the trotter's legacy as a breeder that set him most apart.

All American Standardbred horses can be traced back to a Thoroughbred stallion named Messenger, imported to the United States in 1808. Messenger sired a horse named Abdallah, and Abdallah sired a horse named Hambletonian. From Hambletonian came the four horses from whom every trotting horse competing today has descended: Axworthy, Binden, McKinney, and Peter the Great.

The first colt sired by Peter the Great to go on to racing fame was a filly named Sadie Mac. In 1903 she swept the two-year-old events in the Grand Circuit. Other offspring of Peter the Great have included some of the greatest trotting and pacing horses of all time. Among them:

Greyhound, the world's champion trotter of 1935, who ran the mile in 1:55¼. He was foaled by Elizabeth, one of the last dams of Peter the Great. Due to his light grey coat, he was known as the Grey Glider.

Rosalind, the world's champion mare, who ran a 1:56 ¼ mile in 1939. She was sired by Scotland, the grandson of Peter the Great.

Peter Volo, who was champion in 1912, 1913, and 1914. He was finally beaten as a five-year-old in 1915. Peter Volo in turn sired Volomite, who went on to sire 28 horses who have mile runs under two minutes.

Nibble Hanover, great grandson of Peter the Great, who in 1949 sold for $100,000, the second-highest total ever paid for a trotting stallion.

In all, Peter the Great sired 661 pacing or trotting horses with standard records — meaning 2:30 for trotting or 2:25 for pacing. More Standardbred horses carry the blood of Peter the Great than of any other horse that ever lived. And this is from a horse whose own career as a trotter, or even a work horse, was less than exemplary.

In the last decade of the nineteenth century, Samuel A. Browne, a Scotch-Irishman who operated the Kalamazoo Stock Farms on West Main Street, bought a mare named Lady Duncan for $3000. At first, Browne attempted to use her as a race horse, but she was temperamental and uncontrollable. He put her to work hauling lumber in Northern Michigan, and finally put her to breeding. One of her foals was a mare named Santos.

Santos was purchased by Daniel D. Streeter for $1000 in 1891. Santos was sent to Battle Creek, where she mated with a grey horse named Pilot Medium, grandson of old Hambletonian. The result was a frisky young colt named Peter the Great, named for trainer and driver Peter V. Johnston.

Peter the Great's racing career was a short, struggling endeavor. Like his grandmother, Lady Duncan, Peter the Great was difficult to train and control. In addition, he trotted at uneven gait, improperly balanced. He was often made to wear heavy shoes to correct the imbalance.

For the first three years of his life Peter the Great was largely unnoticed by the racing world. But that world was shocked at the Kentucky Futurity on October 6, 1898. The Kentucky Futurity, held in Lexington, was at the time the greatest race for three-year-olds. Peter the Great set a new record of 2:12 ¼, then considered a splendid time. Suddenly his value skyrocketed, and he was sold by Streeter to wealthy Boston sportsman J. Malcom Forbes for $20,000. He set another mark for the mile at 2:07 ¼. But soon afterwards, Peter the Great went lame, retired from racing, and began his career as a breeder.

Forbes never seemed to fully appreciate the value of Peter the Great. Reportedly, one day while Forbes was driving Peter the Great, the horse slipped on a trolley track, sending horse, carriage, and rider sprawling in the street. In his embarrassment and anger, Forbes relegated Peter the Great to the back of the stable in disgrace. Finally, Forbes sold Peter the Great at the Old Glory Auction in New York to Peter Duryea and William E.D. Stokes for $5000. After the sale, Forbes reportedly said it was the best sale he ever made. His shortsightedness was soon revealed.

Peter the Great was sent to Patchen Wilkes Farm at Lexington, Kentucky, where he stayed until he was 20. Then, in 1915, Peter the Great sold to Greeley Winings for Stoughton A. Fletcher of Indianapolis. Winings paid $50,000 for Peter the Great. It was considered an outrageous figure, and Winings and Fletcher were thought the fools. But by the time Peter the Great died, through sales and breeding fees, he had netted Winings and Fletcher more than $400,000 in profits.

Peter the Great lived at Fletcher's Laurel Hall Farm in Indianapolis until his death in 1923 at the age of 28 years. More than 70 years later, the legacy of Peter the Great can still be found in Standardbred trotters and pacers throughout the modern racing circuit.

SOURCES: "Peter the Great, 2:07 ¼." Kalamazoo: Western Michigan University, 1966. Pp. 5–6. / Pines, Philip A. *The Complete Book of Harness Racing*. New York: Grosset and Dunlap, 1970.

Minnesota

ANIMAL: Sparky
DOB: 1947
DOD: 1963
DESCRIPTION: California sea lion (*Zalophus californus*), approximately 6' long, 400–550 pounds, chocolate brown coat.

Officials from the city of St. Paul, Minnesota, and the Como Zoological Society gathered near the Aquatic Animal Building at the Como Zoo in June of 1989. Their purpose was to dedicate a new amphitheater, representing the culmination of more than three decades of efforts to improve and modernize the zoo. The new facility was called the Sparky Show Amphitheater, a monument to three generations of the Brand-Byng family, and five generations of sea lions named Sparky.

The story of Sparky the sea lion begins in Astoria, Oregon, in 1953. The five-year-old California sea lion, originally from the Sea Lion Caves off the central Oregon Coast, was purchased by Archie Brand. Brand, a Missouri native and former copper miner, bought the sea lion from a man who had owned a restaurant near the Sea Lion Caves and had adopted the animal as a pet. Brand brought Sparky to his truck stop near Astoria, where he first taught him to do tricks.

Brand and his wife, Aili, began displaying the sea lion at boat and water ski shows throughout North America. Sparky would perform tricks such as balancing balls on his nose, standing on his front flippers, and demonstrating mock rescues of children. Immediately, Sparky's intelligence, mischievousness, and playfulness made him a favorite of audiences — especially children. The Sparky the Sea Lion Show became immensely popular. Then, in 1956, at a sports show in Edmonton, Canada, Sparky was spotted by Stanley Hubbard, Sr., owner of radio station KSTP in Minneapolis.

Hubbard had become involved in the project to restore St. Paul's Como Zoo, located in Como Park, which surrounds Lake Como, named for Como Lake in Italy. Hubbard was searching for an attraction for the zoo, something

SPARKY THE SEA LION
(courtesy of Norm Byng)

to rekindle the spark of public interest. Finding his spark in Sparky, he persuaded Archie Brand to bring the Sea Lion Show to St. Paul. Almost 40 years later, it is estimated that more than 35 million animal lovers — spanning four generations from Minnesota and around the world — have seen the Sparky the Sea Lion Show.

California sea lions belong to an order of animals called pinnipeds, which include the odobenids (walruses), the phocids (seals), and the otariids (sea lions). California sea lions are the most common pinnipeds on the Pacific Coast of North America, as well as the most popular performing pinniped. Although sea lions are often referred to as seals, there are many characteristics which differentiate the two families. For example, sea lions have external ear flaps on either side of their heads, while seals have none. Sea lions have reversible rear flippers which enable the animals to "sit upright" on their haunches. Seals cannot reverse their rear flippers, and must always lie on their stomachs. Differences in teeth, whiskers, fur, and other features further distinguish the two pinniped families.

California sea lions are slender and streamlined, with coats of fur ranging in color from buff to chocolate brown. Large males can be as long as eight feet and weigh as much as 700 pounds. The male's most prominent feature is a huge sagittal crest on its forehead; the crest is absent in the female. Tricks performed by sea lions at zoos and aquariums are not new behaviors, but merely adaptions of behaviors demonstrated in the wild.

The Sparky the Sea Lion Show has run continually at the Como Zoo since 1956, while the road show was presented through 1973. When Archie Brand died in 1988, the shows came under the direction of Brand's stepson, Norman Byng and his daughter, Tanya. The original Sparky died in 1963 of pneumonia and has been succeeded by four other Sparky Sea Lions. All have been owned and raised by the Byngs at the Sea Lion farm in Carthage, Missouri. The zoo's otariids live year round in the Aquatic Animal Building, and now perform at the Sparky Show Amphitheater.

In addition to the success he brought to the Byngs, Sparky did indeed spark an interest in the fortunes of Como Zoo. The revenue obtained from the millions of fans drawn by Sparky helped to rejuvenate the zoo, allowing renovation of many of the once dilapidated buildings and enclosures. Today, the Como Zoo and the nearby Minnesota State Zoo work together to bring wildlife and environmental education to the residents of Minnesota. And the fifth-generation Sparky continues to provide laughter and pleasure to audiences at the Sparky Show Amphitheater.

SOURCE: Telephone interview with Norman Byng, February 10, 1995.

Mississippi

ANIMAL: Teddy Bear
DOB: Late 1890s (most likely)
DOD: Probably somewhere between 1910 and 1920
DESCRIPTION: American black bear (*Ursus americanus*), black coat with
   beige snout, approximately 6' long, approximately 300 pounds.

It's the stuff of which legends are made.

One of the most colorful presidents in American history was Theodore Roosevelt. Not only was he the youngest person ever to take the oath of office — 42 years, 10 months — but he was probably the most vigorous. He was a colonel among the Rough Riders of the Spanish-American War, famous for their charge

DRAWING THE LINE IN MISSISSIPPI BY CLIFF BERRYMAN
(courtesy of Washing Star Collection, D.C. Public Library)

up San Juan Hill in Cuba. A well-rounded athlete, he was a fan of pugilism, equestrianism, and other sports. He was an enthusiastic outdoorsman and a strong advocate for conservation. He was also celebrated for his African safaris. No hunting trip along the Congo River, however, caused the stir of one renowned expedition back home, not far from the Mississippi River. On November 4, 1902, President Theodore Roosevelt took a hunting trip through the Delta National Forest outside of Onward, Mississippi, 25 miles north of Vicksburg. Accompanying him was a guide of considerable experience named Holt Collier, who held the leash of a pack of hunting dogs. Entering the woods, the dogs picked up the scent of a black bear. While the president waited at the camp with his entourage, Collier set off after the bear. Little Sunflower River runs through the Delta National Forest, and part of the river drains into a small waterhole. After several hours of tracking, the dogs finally cornered the black bear in the middle of the waterhole.

As the exhausted bear waited in the water, the dogs attacked, lunging one after another toward the bruin. Despite his fatigue, the bear summoned enough strength to kill one of the hounds in the skirmish. Collier watched another of his dogs in the grip of the bear. Realizing that despite their numbers, the dogs were badly outmatched, the guide grabbed his rifle. Not wanting to spoil the hunt for the president, Collier struck the bear several times on the head with the gun barrel, rendering it unconscious.

So the story goes — though at this point it begins to come into question. An adult black bear can stand more than six feet tall on its hind legs and weigh more than 300 pounds. It can crush the skull of a steer with a single blow of its paw. It is difficult to believe that a single man would stand much of a chance of knocking it out with a rifle butt. Unless, of course, the bear was a cub, in which case one wonders why it was pursued and attacked by a whole pack of hunting dogs.

In any case, Collier sent word back to camp for the president to come quickly. Fearing the bear would awake and escape, he tied it to a tree with a stout rope.

Soon Roosevelt arrived at the water hole. The bear had awakened but was still fastened by the rope to the tree. Seeing the bear, Roosevelt declared he had not the heart to shoot the defenseless animal, nor would he allow anyone else in the party to harm it. The bear was set free.

Word of the president's display of mercy and sportsmanship made its way to the press. Stories concerning Roosevelt's hunting expedition were published across the country. Two days later, a cartoon by *Washington Star* political cartoonist Cliff Berryman was released. The cartoon depicted Roosevelt sparing the life of a poor bear cub, with Collier holding the frightened animal on a rope. The cartoon was entitled "Drawing the Line in Mississippi." At this point, the story takes an unexpected twist.

In Brooklyn, New York, a seamstress named Rose Michtom had created two stuffed toy bears. They had light-colored plush fur, their bodies were filled with excelsior stuffing, and two black shirt buttons provided each set of eyes. Morris Michtom, Rose's husband and a stationery store keeper, saw the bears. He had read the Roosevelt hunting story, had seen Berry's cartoon in the newspaper, and was aware of the public attention the episode had drawn. In a moment of inspiration — the kind for which most merchants wait a lifetime — Michtom asked for, and was granted, permission by Teddy Roosevelt himself to name the bears after him. Soon, in Morris Michtom's Brooklyn stationery store window, there appeared an American first: the Teddy Bear.

At the same time, the Germany-based Steiff Company began to produce stuffed toy bears as well. Margarete Steiff, a childhood victim of polio, was a paraplegic with continued weakness in her right hand. Learning to sew, she created a line of stuffed animals, including elephants, horses, camels, and bears.

When Steiff's bears were exhibited at the Leipzig Fair in Germany in 1903, an American buyer, conscious of the Teddy Bear frenzy created in the States, ordered several thousand. Apparently some of these bears served as decorations at the wedding reception of President Roosevelt's daughter, and of course, Roosevelt was delighted with the attention.

Between 1903 and 1907, the total number of Steiff bears produced jumped from 12,000 to 974,000. The Teddy Bear boom was on, and it hasn't died out yet. And it all was due to an obscure black bear in the Delta National Forest near Onward, Mississippi.

Or so the story goes.

SOURCES: Bialosky, Peggy, and Bialosky, Alan. *Teddy Bear Catalog*. New York: Workman, 1980. / "Bear Hunt Reunion to Celebrate Birth of "Teddy Bear" in Onward." *Oxford* (Mississippi) *Eagle*, 1986.

Missouri

ANIMAL: Charlie Chan
DOB: 1967
DOD: July 1986
DESCRIPTION: Alley cat, snow white coat, 18 pounds.

Mrs. Grace Alma Patterson Wiggins of Joplin, Missouri, died on April 29, 1977. According to her last will and testament, the entirety of her estate — worth $262,000 (with interest) and including a three-bedroom pink brick house, a seven-acre pet cemetery, and valuable antiques — was bequeathed to her closest companion. The fortune would belong to that companion alone, provided he abided by a single condition of the will: that he continue to live in the house they occupied together for many years.

Mrs. Wiggins had found her friend huddling in an alleyway in Carthage, Missouri. Wiggins took him in and nursed him back to health. He continued to live with her, even when she moved to 2233 Illinois Avenue in Joplin, some 58 miles west of Springfield. Mrs. Wiggins had no family and no close friends; she explained the will by saying simply, "I like cats better than friends." Charlie Chan was a 11-year-old white alley cat.

The trustees for the estate were Mr. and Mrs. Richard Webb, whose job was to make certain that all of Charlie Chan's needs were met. This meant it was up to the Webbs to be sure there was always someone around the house to provide for the alley cat.

At first, Mrs. Wiggins' neighbors tried to care for Charlie Chan. Mrs. Fenix would make two trips a day to the Chan estate to make the sure the cat was fed and the litter box was emptied. Finally, other obligations pressed on her time, and another arrangement was made.

A young couple soon moved into the Illinois Avenue estate to watch over the cat. The husband's business transactions forced them to move to another location, and a third caretaker was sought.

This time a 30-year-old schoolteacher named Colleen O'Flaherty moved in to watch over Charlie Chan. For three years — from 1980 through 1983 — O'Flaherty was provided residence in the house, in exchange for a $35 monthly utility payment and the feeding and care of the feline.

O'Flaherty referred to Charlie Chan as a great and intelligent cat. She once said that he loved people — "If a new person comes in, he'll cuddle up and try to make friends" — but he tended to shun the other cats. At one point, Charlie gained an inordinate amount of weight, and O'Flaherty had to maintain him on a strict diet — rigors of the job, apparently.

Lee and Barbara Belle were Charlie's final caretakers. He died of kidney failure in 1986. No foul play is suspected.

Not surprisingly, a lot of attention was focused on the house at 2233 Illinois Avenue, particularly by the media and the curious. Colleen O'Flaherty said her brother-in-law used to kid her for living in a "cat house." In 1985, the *Guinness Book of World Records* listed Charlie Chan as the world's richest cat.

At Charlie Chan's death, provisions in the will stated, the estate would be auctioned off and proceeds would go to local and national humane societies. Mrs. Wiggins, an avid animal lover, had promised the funds to the National Anti-Vivisection Society in Chicago, the Humane Society of the United States in Washington, D.C., and the Humane Family Foundation of Connecticut. But even after Charlie Chan's death, the fur continued to fly.

The Anti-Vivisection Society and the Humane Society of the United States contended in court that the Humane Family Foundation could not be considered a beneficiary. The will, they contended, had originally designated Humane Information Services, Inc., of St. Petersburg, Florida, as the third beneficiary. But Humane Information Services merged with the American Humane Foundation for Children in 1985 to become the Humane Family Foundation. Thus, contended the first two beneficiaries, the third beneficiary actually no longer existed. This promised to be a cat fight of highest order (the results of which the author has been unable to determine at the date of this book's publication).

One neighbor said, "Maybe the neighborhood can finally get back to normal, now that we don't have a cat owning a house here." Now that Charlie is gone, perhaps the residents of Illinois Street in Joplin, Missouri, have a chance for an uneventful life. But then, what fun will that be?

SOURCES: Attoun, Marti. "Late Feline's Estate to Benefit Humane Society, 2 Other Groups." *Joplin Globe*, August 30, 1986. / Campbell, Susan. "Charlie Chan Is Sitting Pretty." *Joplin Globe*, June 17, 1979. / *Guinness Book of World Records*. New York: Sterling, 1985. P. 54. / Woodin, Debby. "Fur Flies as Fight Over Fluffy Feline's Fortune Fans Lawsuit." *Joplin Globe*, December 6, 1986.

Montana

ANIMAL: Shep
DOB: Probably 1930
DOD: January 1942
DESCRIPTION: Shetland sheepdog, black, white, and tan coat, 13–16" tall at shoulder, 27 pounds.

No one really knows where Shep called home. Those who worked around the railroad station at Fort Benton presumed he lived somewhere in the hills surrounding the area, but no one knew for sure.

No one really knew how old he was, either. Given the average lifespan of a Shetland sheepdog, the guess was he was around seven years old when he started visiting the train station. Again, no one knew for sure, just as no one knew his master. All anyone could say was that in 1936, a train from Fort Benton took the body of an unknown, unheralded shepherd to an unknown burial site. A mangy mutt of a sheepdog — no doubt a Shetland, but also no doubt some other breed — watched the train go and, apparently, expected the master to return. But the master, whoever he was, never did.

Long thought to be collies in miniature, Shetland sheepdogs were bred from small border collies and transported to the Shetland Islands off the coast of Scotland. These islands, made of rugged rock with sparse vegetation, are regularly battered by fierce gales and storms. Any animal that could learn to live there would have to be small, lightweight, tough as nails, adaptable, and clever — in short, a survivor. This is the story of one such individual.

For five years, like a ghost haunting its homestead, Shep awaited the master's return to the train station. From somewhere in the hills surrounding, the sheepdog would somehow sense the approach of the next train. He would look down from the hills, no doubt bark expectantly, and sprint to the station. He would wait patiently as the train rolled to a stop. Tired passengers would disembark to find a bedraggled sheepdog at their heels, sniffing and snooping, looking for his master. But of course, Shep would not find him; he would trot away from each passenger and on to the next until the train pulled away. Then, apparently, he would return to the hills to await the arrival of the next coach.

It is not quite known how the sheepdog survived on his own. It is presumed that he foraged and scavenged for himself in the hills. He was known to drink from the Missouri River, which flowed below the station. Eventually he dug a hole under the train station building and began living there. Soon local residents — those who worked at the station, and those who lived near it — started leaving food and water for the sheepdog, which he seemed to welcome. P.J. McSweeny, the section foreman for the station, would offer him scraps of food, and after a time, McSweeny's house became a regular stop for Shep at Fort Benton.

The beginning of 1942 was a lonely, uncertain time in northwest Montana — indeed throughout much of the world. World War II was well into its fourth year; America had just been attacked a month earlier by the Japanese empire. Young men began going off to war, and residents began looking for diversions from the horrors that seemed to engulf all of humanity. In northwest Montana, they found their diversion in a little dog.

Word began to travel about this unusual sheepdog, who came to symbolize loyalty and steadfastness. Stories about him spread throughout the countryside and eventually landed in local newspapers and magazines. His legend spread to other newspapers, then began to touch the hearts of readers in Europe and around the world. *Ripley's Believe It or Not* even featured Shep in a cartoon, which further advanced his fame.

No one knew how long Shep's search for his master would continue. By January of 1942, Shep was 12 years old, and his years of scrounging and living on his own had taken their toll. The bounce had long left his step, his eyesight was failing, and he was hard of hearing. On one fateful day, when Shep saw the next train rumbling toward the station, he pushed his weary body forward, leaping onto the tracks, trying to cross to the other side. Shep's foot slipped on the iron rails, and the dog fell as the engine roared upon him. Shep was crushed to death.

Shep was buried on a hillside overlooking the Fort Benton train station. Among the mourners were McSweeney, station agent A.V. Schanche, and Mayor E.L. Shields of Great Falls, Montana — who was once a conductor for one of the trains that stopped at Fort Benton. William Jones, a station employee, constructed Shep's coffin and drove it to the gravesite in his truck. A bugler from the Fort Benton Boy Scout Troop played Taps over the grave, while a local minister gave the eulogy.

The eulogy's theme was a tribute to faithfulness.

SOURCE: "Shep Dies Still Waiting for Master's Return." *Great Falls Tribune*, January 25, 1942.

ANIMAL: Big Medicine
DOB: May 3, 1933
DOD: August 25, 1959
DESCRIPTION: American Bison or buffalo (*Bison bison*), white hide, tan hoofs, brown cap, 12' long, 1900 pounds.

Numbering more than 60,000,000 before European settlers came to North America, the American bison — also called buffalo — traveled in herds from the Eastern seaboard to the Rocky Mountains, from Northern Canada

BIG MEDICINE
(courtesy of Montana Historical Society, Helena)

well into Mexico. But so devastating was the white man's plan to control the Plains Indians tribes by eradicating the buffalo that the great animals numbered fewer than 600 in 1889. Since albino bison appear on the average only once among every 5,000,000 births, most people assumed that a white buffalo would never be born in North America again.

Yet on May 3, 1933, at the National Bison Range near Moiese, Montana (about 30 miles north of Missoula), a white buffalo calf was born. Not a true albino, the calf had slightly pigmented, light blue eyes, rather than pink. Its hooves were tan rather than white, and at the top of its white head it sported a dark brown cap.

Originally (and unimaginatively) dubbed Whitey, the buffalo was eventually renamed to honor his significance to Native Americans. The history of the buffalo and Native Americans is inextricably intermixed. They used the buffalo for food, clothing, shelter, fuel, tools, and virtually every other aspect of their existence. Yet, despite regular hunting of the bison, the impact of Native Americans on the population of the beasts was minimal — particularly in comparison to the devastation brought about by the Europeans.

The Blackfoot tribe held special spiritual reverence for the white buffalo, considering it the property of the sun. The man who killed the white buffalo would be given the power of the sun, and the good medicine of the white bison would be passed on from the buffalo hide to the warrior, his family, and his tribe. In honor of this tradition, Whitey was renamed Big Medicine.

Big Medicine stood six feet at hump, weighed more than 1900 pounds, and was 12 feet long. This beautiful and unusual animal attracted worldwide attention and became the staple attraction of the National Bison Range. Big Medicine sired numerous offspring, including "Little Medicine," a deaf and blind true albino, in 1937. Little Medicine was taken to National Zoological Gardens in Washington, D.C., where he lived for 12 years.

A true native son of Montana, Big Medicine spent his entire life on the National Bison Range. During his latter days, the white buffalo lived on the range's smaller exhibition pasture, where he received special attention in an effort to prolong his life. During his last three years, Big Medicine ate a special diet of steamed barley in molasses, high-protein rabbit pellets, two brands of bran, and cut alfalfa. Despite the constant care and special diet, Big Medicine's weight dropped dramatically, until on August 25, 1959, he died on the range where he was born.

The bison's hide was shipped to Jonas Brothers in Denver, Colorado, where it was tanned. The hide then traveled to Browning, Montana, to be mounted by renowned sculptor and taxidermist Bob Scriver. Governor Donald G. Nutter dedicated the mounted work at the Montana Historical Society on July 13, 1961. Big Medicine stands there today, where he is visited by more than 100,000 annually.

Since the turn of the century — no doubt partly due to the study of animals such as Big Medicine — great strides have been made to save the American bison from extinction. Projects such as the Tallgrass Prairie Preserve in north-central Oklahoma have set aside vast expanses of acreage in order to repopulate the buffalo herds and return areas of the Great Plains to their once majestic state. At Tallgrass, for example, the environmental organization known as the Nature Conservancy has purchased more than 36,000 acres on which grass species attractive to the buffalo, such as foxtail barley, will be allowed to return to their once plentiful harvest. The buffalo will be gradually reintroduced to the renewed grasslands. These kinds of efforts have done much to bring the buffalo — whose population now numbers more than 30,000 — away from the brink of elimination.

SOURCES: Froman, Robert. "The Buffalo That Refused to Vanish." *Marvels & Mysteries of Our Animal World*. Pleasantville, N.Y.: Reader's Digest Association, 1964. Pp. 59–62. / Montana Historical Society news release, n.d.

Nebraska

ANIMAL: Old Charlie
DOB: 1866
DOD: May 17, 1888
DESCRIPTION: Kentucky saddle horse (*Equus caballus*), dark brown coat with white around hooves, approximately 16 hands high.

For the title of "Greatest Showman of the nineteenth century," the only rival to the great P.T. Barnum might be William Frederick "Buffalo Bill" Cody. His

OLD CHARLIE
(courtesy of Buffalo Bill Historical Center, Cody, WY)

colossal Wild West Show, organized in 1883, was an international favorite, playing to more than six million people in 34 years. The Wild West Show featured shooting exhibitions, buffalo hunting, a stagecoach capture, and a Pony Express ride, and it captivated audiences throughout nineteenth century America.

The image of Buffalo Bill burned into the American consciousness is that of a long-haired, golden-bearded, hat-waving cowboy on his horse. The horse in that image could very well be Old Charlie, Buffalo Bill's favorite mount. Cody rode with Old Charlie from 1873 to 1888, and Old Charlie became the most publicized horse of his day. During that time Cody owned a ranch outside North Platte, Nebraska. The ranch served as the winter home and headquarters for Buffalo Bill's Wild West Show, as well as home for Old Charlie. It has since been transformed into Buffalo Bill Ranch State Historic Park.

William Frederick Cody was born on February 26, 1846, in Scott County, Iowa, and died January 10, 1917, in Denver, Colorado. Cody gained fame as a Pony Express rider, a horse wrangler, and a hunter. He gained his name while hunting buffalo for the Union Pacific Railroad workers at Fort Ellsworth, Kansas. In eight months, he is said to have slaughtered 4280 head of buffalo, a feat that won him the title of greatest buffalo hunter on the Great Plains. Although it brought fame to the name of "Buffalo Bill," such widespread, wholesale slaughter — which became common on the Great Plains in the nineteenth century — led the American bison to the very brink of extinction. In 1889 there were fewer than 600 bison left of herds that had once easily numbered in the millions. Only through careful preservation has the bison returned to a population of several thousand.

It was in the 1870s that Cody gained fame as an Indian fighter. Old Charlie was with him in 1876 during the much-publicized scalping of the Cheyenne Indian sub-chief Yellow Hair.

In 1883, Cody organized the Wild West Show, which he presented to enthusiastic audiences throughout the United States. Huge throngs turned out to watch the extravaganza, as many as 40,000 per show. His show featured sharpshooting Annie Oakley, and the stoic Sioux chief Sitting Bull, who specialized in recreating the story of Custer's Last Stand. Members of the audience included such notables as President Grover Cleveland, General William T. Sherman, Mark Twain, and P.T. Barnum himself. Buffalo Bill would greet the cheering crowds, proudly astride Old Charlie, his golden hair flowing in the breeze, his hat waving toward the sky.

Having conquered the United States from shore to shore, Cody took the Wild West Show to Europe in 1887. It was on this trip that Old Charlie received the most acclaim. While in London, Charlie caught the attention of Grand Duke Michale of Russia, cousin of the Grand Duke Alexis. So taken by the stallion was he, that the Grand Duke Michale was heard to comment on the superior horsemanship of America. Charlie's owner beamed with pride.

Unfortunately, on the voyage home from Europe, Old Charlie took ill. Aboard the *Persian Monarch*, Buffalo Bill sat by Old Charlie's side as the steed's health rapidly failed. Finally, on May 18, 1888, the end came. In a moving tribute, Cody recalls the final moments:

> The death of a human being could not have excited more real mourning. Everyone had some reminiscence of Old Charlie's Sagacity, and many an eye was moist with tears. His burial was appointed for 8:00 in the evening. I should have preferred to carry him back home and bury him on the prairie, but that was impossible. During the day he lay in state on the deck, decently wrapped in a canvas shroud and covered with the Stars and Stripes. At the appointed hour the entire ship's company assembled. The band played "Auld Lang Syne," lights were burned, and as the faithful creature glided into the water, the ships cannon boomed a last farewell to my consistent friend and companion for the last 15 years.

SOURCES: Froman, Robert. "The Buffalo That Refused to Vanish." *Marvels & Mysteries of Our Animal World.* Pleasantville, N.Y.: Reader's Digest Association, 1964. Pp. 59–62. / Yost, Nellie Snyder. *Buffalo Bill: His Family, His Friends, Fame, Failures, and Fortunes.* Athens, Oh.: Swallow, 1979.

Nevada

ANIMAL: The Tonopah Burro
DOB: Probably 1897
DOD: Around 1910
DESCRIPTION: Burro (*Equus asinus*), approximately 10 hands high, dark
    brown coat.

JIM BUTLER AND BURRO
(courtesy of Nevada Historical Society)

A cold wind ripped through the campground that the Shoshone Indians called Tonopah, meaning "Little Spring." Big Jim Butler — all six feet and 225 pounds of him — had been prospecting along the San Antonio Range in Nye County, Nevada. It was May 17, 1900. Butler would rest here for a couple of nights and start out fresh the following morning.

During the night of May 18, as Butler huddled in his tent, the bitter desert wind blew even harder, moaning up and down the grounds of the camp. One of Butler's burros wandered in the dark from where it stood in search of better shelter from the cold. Finally, it settled under the shelf of an overhanging ledge on Mount Oddie. The shelf provided some protection from wind, and the burro was finally able to find comfort.

When Butler awoke the next morning, he spent a considerable amount of time stumbling through the sandstorm, searching for his prodigal donkey. Finally, he spotted the burro a substantial distance outside the camp. The wind was blowing fiercely as ever, so Butler joined the burro under the ledge, waiting for the blasts to subside.

Butler grew bored and impatient as he waited. Restlessly, he struck his pick into the ground below the ledge, not far from where the burro stood. The samples he unearthed looked so promising that he packed them away to have them appraised later.

The samples, which Butler had originally guessed to be black iron, turned out to be part of a rich deposit of silver and gold. An assay of the sample revealed 395 ounces of silver and 15 ounces of gold. The vein was destined to become one of the richest in Nevada. Butler eventually established several mines around Tonopah, and one of them he named the Burro Mine, after the creature who led him to it.

Butler's discovery could not have been better timed, as a depressed Nevada looked for a reason to be optimistic. The mines of Virginia City and other areas had been dry and vacant for 20 years. With the emigration of many once-eager miners, Nevada's population had been waning for several years and now depended on its relatively meager agricultural industry.

Butler was a native of California and the son of a prospector. He had settled in a Nevada town called Belmont and owned the Little Antelope Ranch just outside of town. Although Butler had been elected district attorney and superintendent of schools in Belmont (then the Nye County seat), he could never shake his inherited love of mining, and he continued prospecting when away from his other duties.

According to history, the burro at the heart of this story had never been named. Burros are actually derived from African wild asses, which are native to the desert areas of Ethiopia and east Africa. They were brought to the new world by Spaniards in the 1500s and have been used in prospecting ever since. They are hardy and surefooted, and their ability to survive on little food and water make them ideal pack animals in severe environments. They were used to carry the miners' tools, bedding, food, and sometimes the miners themselves. Some historians have asserted that the expansion of the American West has as much to do with these little donkeys as with any other domesticated animal.

Other Tonopah mines claimed by Butler and his wife, Belle, included the Desert Queen and the Mizpah. Belle Butler used to cook the meals and haul the water for the miners' camp at Mizpah, which is now the site of the Mizpah Hotel in Tonopah.

SOURCES: Brown, Mrs. Hugh. *Lady in Boomtown*. Reno and Las Vegas: University of Nevada Press, 1991. / Paher, Stanley W. *Tonopah: Silver Camp of Nevada*. Las Vegas: Nevada Publications, 1986. / Svendsen, Elisabeth D. *A Passion for Donkeys*. London: David & Charles, 1980. Pp. 11–13.

New Hampshire

ANIMAL: Chinook
DOB: 1917
DOD: 1928
DESCRIPTION: Sled dog, light brown coat, German shepherd face with floppy ears, approximately 27 inches tall.

In 1917 Arthur Treadwell Walden, a New Hampshire adventurer who had been a dog-sled mail and freight driver in the Klondike, created the only sled dog breed native to New England. At a farm in a small village named

Wonalancet in New Hampshire, where Walden had raised and trained many mongrels to pull sleds, he mated a male stray husky found near the Canadian border with a female German shepherd — the granddaughter of one of Admiral Perry's sled dogs, who took the admiral to the North Pole.

The result was three identical puppies, the largest and strongest of which was dubbed Chinook. Chinook was reputed to be a genius among dogs. When in the city, for example, it is told that Chinook would notice and obey the signals of the traffic cops at the intersections. He became famous, and the leader among dogs at Wonalancet Farm. At one point Chinook led a team that brought electricity to Wonalancet, hauling wire and poles and tools through snowbound woods that neither horse nor oxen nor tractor would have been able to cross.

Chinook quickly gained attention as one of the largest, strongest, and smartest of sled dogs, and Walden began mating Chinook with female dogs of predominantly German shepherd background. The resulting puppies grew to be large, tawny dogs that looked as if they all came from the same mold, each generation identical to the last. They looked much like yellow-brown German shepherds, but with floppy ears. The Chinook breed, as it came to be known, quickly grew in popularity.

Chinooks made their first real mark in dogsled races in 1922. The Brown Paper Company of Berlin, New Hampshire, sponsored the first Eastern International Sled Dog Derby. Arthur Walden, with a team of six dogs led by Chinook, won the three-day race. Later that year, the same team became the first sled dogs to climb Mt. Washington, 4775 feet above sea level in New Hampshire.

In 1931, in a publicity contest for a dog food company, a Massachusetts boy named Lawrence Orne and a Chinook dog named Nashua were named "America's Most Typical Boy and Dog." Unfortunately, by that time the Chinook's fame as a sled dog had begun to drag as the breed faced stiff competition from smaller, speedier dogs from Alaska and Canada.

As for the original Chinook, he met his demise in 1928. Chinook had accompanied Arthur Walden on Admiral Byrd's first expedition to the Antarctic. Walden brought a number of dogs from Wonalancet Farm to pull the sleds of the expedition. While Chinook, at the ripe old age of 11, was beyond the years at which he could be depended upon for sled pulling, he was allowed to run alongside the other dogs.

Then he disappeared. Admiral Byrd recalled the incident:

> An incident, perhaps the saddest during our whole stay in the Antarctic, was the loss of Walden's famous lead dog, Chinook. Chinook was Walden's pride, and there was no doubting the fact he was a great dog....
> ...A few days after his twelfth birthday, he disappeared. We searched the camp for him, without success; in the trampled snow about the ship, it was impossible to find his tracks. ... All this was a deep disappointment to Walden, who wanted to bury Chinook in his harness.

Although Chinook's body was never recovered, scratches were much later discovered on the edge of a deep crevasse. It was theorized that perhaps Chinook had fallen into the crevasse and had spent several days trying to climb out, finally succumbing to exhaustion or starvation or both. The truth, of course, will be never known.

Chinook's disappearance became front-page news around the world. Arthur Walden returned to New Hampshire to a hero's welcome. Many of the residents around Wonalancet proposed to rename a road "Walden Highway" in his honor. Walden declined, insisting the road be called Chinook Trail. To this day, the section of Highway 113A between Wonalancet and Tamworth goes by that name.

Since its heyday in the 1920s, the Chinook breed has taken a nose dive among dog owners. Never recognized as an official breed by the American Kennel Club, the Chinook has continued to dwell precariously near extinction. In 1966 the *Guinness Book of World Records* declared it the world's rarest dog breed, and current estimates put the entire world's population below 90 dogs. The future of this uniquely American dog is in grave jeopardy.

But the likeness of the original Chinook is still quite popular in central New Hampshire. It can be seen on road signs all along Highway 113A, between Tamworth and Wonalancet.

SOURCES: Flamholtz, Cathy J. *A Celebration of Rare Breeds.* Ft. Payne, Ala.: OTR, 1986. / Harkness, Marjory Gane. *The Tamworth Narrative.* Freeport, Maine: Bond Wheelwright, 1958. / *The Inventive Yankee.* Dublin, N.H.: Yankee, 1989.

New Jersey

ANIMAL: Taro
DOB: 1989
DOD: Still alive
DESCRIPTION: Akita dog, black and white with dark face, 110 pounds, 27" tall at shoulders.

In the movies, death row is traditionally presented as a long line of dimly lit prison cells, bisected by a long, narrow corridor. The corridor leads to an ominous-looking chamber, and convicts are marched toward the chamber by a somber guard and a mumbling priest. Wailing and gnashing can be heard echoing off the prison cell walls.

For Taro, the Death-Row Akita, the end was not quite so dramatic. Yet his story is no less controversial than many a Hollywood gangster film.

Taro's predicament was predicated by a law passed by the New Jersey legislature in 1987. The "Vicious Dog" Law (A-4439), sponsored by Assemblyman

Joseph Azzolino, defines a "vicious dog" as any dog which "even when unprovoked, approaches, in a threatening or terrorizing manner, any person in apparent attitude of attack upon the streets, sidewalks, or any public grounds or places, or any dog with a known propensity, tendency, or disposition to attack without provocation, to cause injury, or otherwise endanger the safety of human beings or domestic animals." The law also allows that an animal control officer may impound such a dog if it attacks and wounds a human being or domestic animal, and provides that the dog may be destroyed after a five-day waiting period.

Akitas were originally bred as hunting dogs in seventeenth century Northern Japan. These dogs have always been known for their combination of dignity, good nature, alert courage, and docility. Helen Keller is credited with bringing the first akitas to the United States. She was presented with a two-month-old puppy as a gift from the Minister of Education in Japan.

The attributes of akitas makes the incident which led to "The Death Row Akita Story" that much more disputable. One version of the December 25, 1990, occurrence says that ten-year-old Brie Halfond, niece of Taro's owners Lonnie and Sandy Lehrer, entered the Lehrers' bedroom while at a family gathering in Haworth. Taro attacked the girl, biting her on the lower lip. Doctors and police who treated the girl comfirmed it was a bite.

The Lehrers, on the other hand, claim that Taro could not have bitten the girl, as a bite would have left a much more severe wound. They claim the dog must have scratched the lip with a front paw. The Lehrers assert that there had been no official record of Taro ever attacking a human being (although Taro had attacked three dogs, killing one). They also claimed that their own kids' friends had played with Taro on numerous occasions with no danger to themselves.

In any case, Taro was impounded and quarantined, and in early 1991 it was decided the akita should be destroyed. A municipal judge agreed and, upon appeal, so did a superior court judge. Undaunted, the Lehrers appealed the case again, this time to the New Jersey State Appellate Court.

As lawyers debated the case, Taro was housed in the jail kennel, and the costs of the case continued to escalate. By 1993, the costs attributed to the case were estimated as follows:

> Prosecution Costs = $ 60,000
> Defense Costs = $ 25,000
> Jail Kennel Bill = $ 18,000
> (includes $2.50 per day in dog food)
> _____
> TOTAL = $103,000

In total, Taro spent more than 1000 days on death row. In the meantime, various factions debated the morality of the case. Predictably, taxpayers were outraged at the bill, footed mostly by their hard-earned money. Animal rights activists as celebrated as Brigitte Bardot entered the fray, many complaining that hardened criminals in jail for rape or robbery were being released sooner than Taro.

The case moved further up the judicial ladder when the appellate court decided to uphold the execution of Taro. In mid–January 1994, the State Supreme Court refused to review the case, and the execution order was set for March 1.

Finally, after considerable — and understandable — reluctance toward getting involved in this matter, newly elected New Jersey governor Christine Todd Whitman settled the matter. On January 29, 1994, Whitman ordered that the dog should go free, but that it must leave the state permanently. The death sentence was lifted in favor of exile. In a savory bit of understatement, Governor Whitman exclaimed, "This has been going on long enough. It's time to move on."

At last word, Taro had been moved to another state with a couple well versed in the care of akitas. The identity of the couple has remained anonymous, however, to keep the relentless media at bay. The dog is presumed alive and well. Thus, the story of the Death-Row Akita has apparently wound down to a peaceful — and, one hopes, an uneventful — conclusion.

SOURCES: Gray, Jerry. "Dog's Death Sentence Is Reduced to Exile." *New York Times*, 1/29/94, vol. 143, issue 49491. P. 1. / Hanley, Robert. "For New Jersey Dog, 1000 Days on Death Row." *New York Times*, 10/14/93, vol. 143, issue 49484. P. B1.

New Mexico

ANIMAL: Smokey Bear
DOB: 1942
DOD: 1976
DESCRIPTION: Black bear (*Ursus americanus*), approximately 6' tall, approximately 400 pounds.

Is there an American man, woman, or child — anyone who has camped out sometime in the last 40 years — who would fail to recognize the figure of Smokey Bear? Since 1950, he has addressed Americans from roadside billboards, warning, "Only you can prevent forest fires." On television, he has protected little animals and snuffed out smoldering cigarettes. He has become the symbol of the National Forest Service, of fire prevention, and of camping throughout the United States.

Camping as an organized, popular recreational activity probably began around the turn of the century. Of course, individuals had camped in the

THE REAL SMOKEY BEAR
(courtesy of Brenda Clymire, Photo Archives,
National Zoological Park, Smithsonian Institution)

wilderness for years before that time. But as the nineteenth century came to a close, organizations such as the Adirondack Mountain Club, the Appalachian Mountain Club, and the Sierra Club came into being. As leisure activities came into greater prominence as the twentieth century progressed, camping became a weekend and holiday pastime for millions of Americans.

Efforts toward forest fire prevention did not begin because of an increased interest in camping. During World War II, the American war effort depended largely upon timber from the California coast and Pacific Northwest. Timber was used to produce cargo ships, gun stocks, and many more military items. In a move to sabotage some of that war effort, a Japanese submarine shelled portions of the California coast, engulfing forest acres and destroying potential timber sources.

In 1942, in an effort to increase public awareness about the danger of such attacks — and of forest fires in general — the United States Forest Service launched a campaign called the Cooperative Forest Fire Prevention Program.

The goal was to distribute educational posters among civilians throughout the United States. There was just one problem: the program needed a symbol.

At first the symbol was going to be Bambi the deer, after the 1929 novel that became a Disney movie (which featured a huge forest fire). But the Forest Service decided to look for an original symbol instead, and in 1944, artist Albert Staehles created the first poster of Smokey the Bear. The Forest Service had its symbol; before long, the symbol would come to life.

On May 4, 1942, a huge fire broke out near Capitan Gap in Lincoln National Forest, near the village of Capitan, New Mexico, some 150 miles southeast of Albuquerque. By May 8, more than 17,000 acres of forest had been destroyed by the flames, some of which had been churned by winds reaching speeds of 70 miles per hour.

To fight the blaze, the Department of Fish and Game organized a crew consisting of volunteers and soldiers from nearby Fort Bliss. The crew, led by Fish and Game officer Speed Simmons, barely escaped being engulfed by the flames themselves, by lying flat upon the forest floor and dousing themselves with canteen water. After this terrifying ordeal the crew found their way back to their camp, and headed out the next day, May 9, to grapple anew with the fire.

As they returned to camp at the end of the day, one of the crewmen spotted a small black bear cub, clinging terror-stricken to the upper trunk of a withered tree. All around were the remains of a charred forest; apparently the cub had wrapped itself around the tree and remained there as the flames roared by. With no mother bear to be found, Simmons sent some of the crew to bring the bear down and take it back to camp. The bear's wounds were covered with salve and bandaged. Crew members fed the cub milk from a bottle and fashioned a bed from a crate.

The next morning, May 10, a Fish and Game officer named Ray Bell took the cub into Santa Fe to see the veterinarian, Dr. E.J. Smith. Smith kept the cub for a week, after which he complained that so many people had come to see the poor baby bear, he could hardly get any work done. Ray Bell eventually took the cub home, where it was cared for by Bell's family.

Before long, the United States Forest Service caught wind of the story of the black bear cub and decided to make the bear the living symbol of its Cooperative Forest Fire Prevention Program. By 1950, the bear cub had been named Smokey, and he had been whisked away to Washington, D.C., where, on June 30, 1950, he officially took up his role as chief spokes-animal for the Forest Service.

Smokey continued to live in Washington until 1976, when he died of old age at the National Zoo. Smokey's body was flown back to the village of Capitan, where it was buried at Smokey Bear State Historic Park. The park, created in the 1950s, featured the Smokey Bear Museum to commemorate Smokey

Bear's life, legend, and message. In 1994, the residents of Capitan hosted a celebration of the fiftieth anniversary of Smokey Bear as the symbol of the United States Forest Service.

SOURCES: DeLeon-Stallings, Dianne. "Happy Birthday, Smokey: Our Favorite Cub Turns 50." *New Mexico Magazine*, July 1994. Pp. 84–89. / Guck, Dorothy. "The Tale of Smokey Bear." *New Mexico Wildlife*, May/June 1994. P. 10.

New York

ANIMAL: Fala
DOB: 1934
DOD: 1952
DESCRIPTION: Scotch terrier, 10" high at shoulder, 19 pounds, black coat.

Fala is, without a doubt, the most famous Scotch terrier in history. For the last five years of Franklin Delano Roosevelt's presidency and life, Fala was his pet, his traveling companion, his solace, and seemingly, his spiritual advisor. Formally named Murray the Outlaw of Fala Hill (for a distant Roosevelt ancestor), this little black Scottie became a small but stalwart figure in the Roosevelt clan.

Fala was presented to Franklin Roosevelt in 1940 by his cousin Margaret Suckley. From the outset, Fala was Roosevelt's constant companion, his little black body serving almost as a shadow. He slept in the president's bedroom, and the two breakfasted regularly together. In fact, word was that Roosevelt would order only the breakfast foods — such as eggs, muffin, ham, or bacon — that Fala would eat.

Fala followed Roosevelt through the White House halls and accompanied him on trips to the Capitol. He also served as a travel companion. He was with the president in 1941 when he conferred with British prime minister Winston Churchill aboard the U.S.S. *Augusta* at Newfoundland. He was with Roosevelt on many occasions. He toured the U.S.S. *Baltimore* in July 1944. Over the three day visit, so many sailors aboard the *Baltimore* sought locks from Fala's coat as souvenirs that the poor scottie was nearly bald by the time he and president disembarked.

September 23, 1944, brought Fala's finest moment. Republican presidential candidate Thomas E. Dewey, governor of New York, had been critical of Roosevelt's performance as commander-in-chief. He leveled charges of wastefulness, corruption, and even nepotism (since two of Roosevelt's sons had become high-ranking military officers). As it turned out, Dewey had made two critical errors: he had criticized the president of the United States during wartime (historically the time when the president has appeared most infallible in the eyes of the American public), and perhaps more consequentially, he criticized the president's dog.

FALA
(courtesy of Franklin D. Roosevelt Library)

In a nationally-broadcast speech before the Teamster's Union, Roosevelt responded:

> What the Republican leaders are now saying is in effect this: "Oh, just forget what we used to say, we have changed our minds now — we have been reading the public opinion polls about these things, and now we know what the American people want." And they say: "Don't leave the task of making peace to those old men who first urged it, and who have already laid the foundation for it, and who have had to fight all of us inch by inch during the last five years to do it. Why, just turn it all over to us. We'll do it skillfully — and we won't lose a single isolationist vote or a single isolationist campaign contribution...."
>
> These Republican leaders have not been content with attacks on me, or my wife, or my sons. No, not content with that, they now include my little dog, Fala. Well, of course, I don't resent attacks, and my family doesn't resent attacks, but Fala does resent attacks. You know, Fala is Scotch, and being a Scottie, as soon as he learned the Republican fiction writers in Congress and out had concocted a story that I had left him behind on the Aleutian Islands and had sent a destroyer back to find him — at a cost to the taxpayer of two or three, or eight or twenty million dollars — his Scotch soul was furious. He has not been the same dog since. I am accustomed to hearing malicious falsehoods about myself — such as that old, worm-eaten chestnut that I have represented myself

as indispensable. But I think I have a right to resent, to object to libelous statements about my dog.

The Teamsters howled, the national audience roared, and once against Roosevelt, the master orator, had conquered the moment. The press went crazy over the speech, what many now consider Roosevelt's very finest. The 1944 presidential campaign would henceforth be known as "Dewey vs. Fala." In one brilliant moment, Roosevelt had side-swiped Dewey's self-assured campaign and transformed the Republican Party into a public laughing-stock. Dewey never recovered, and Roosevelt assured himself an unprecedented fourth straight presidential term.

Fala was in Warm Springs, Georgia, on April 5, 1945, when Franklin Delano Roosevelt collapsed and died from a cerebral hemorrhage. The little Scottie reacted in a manner that could be characterized only as utter despair:

> No one had paid any attention to Fala. He had been dozing in a corner of the room. For a reason beyond understanding, he ran directly for the front screen door and bashed his black head against it. The screen broke and he crawled through and ran snapping and barking up into the hills. There, Secret Service men could see him, standing alone, unmoving, on an eminence. This led to the quiet question: "Do dogs really know?" [Bishop, P. 541]

Fala lived for another seven years (until 1952), bringing comfort and companionship to Eleanor Roosevelt and her staff. But every once in a while, Fala could be seen sitting in some familiar spot, such as near the door of the dining room at Hyde Park, as though expecting Roosevelt to appear and take him along on some important presidential function.

SOURCES: Bishop, Jim. *FDR's Last Year.* New York: William Morrow, 1974. Pp. 540–541. / Hersham, Stella K. *A Woman of Quality: Eleanor Roosevelt.* New York: Crown, 1970. Pp. 74–75. / Lash, Joseph P. *Eleanor: The Years Alone.* New York: W.W. Norton, 1972. Pp. 23, 175–176. / Nash, Gerald D., ed. *Franklin Delano Roosevelt.* Englewood Cliffs, N.J.: Prentice-Hall, 1967. Pp. 66–68. / Tremain, Ruthven. *The Animals' Who's Who.* New York: Charles Scribner's Sons, 1985.

North Carolina

ANIMAL: Mildred
DOB: February 1966
DOD: January 1, 1993
DESCRIPTION: American black bear (*Ursus americanus*), deep black coat, approximately 6' tall, 400 pounds.

MILDRED THE BEAR
(courtesy of Hugh Morton, Grandfather Mountain)

A very unusual bear arrived at North Carolina's Grandfather Mountain Resort in 1968. The bear was unusual, first of all, because her name was Mildred. Not that Mildred is an unusual name; it's just unusual for a bear.

She had been brought to Grandfather Mountain to be released in the wild in order to help repopulate the park with black bears. American black bears had virtually disappeared in North Carolina, and it was hoped that Mildred would begin to turn the tide. Attempts to turn her loose in the wild, however, revealed a second very unusual trait in Mildred. She apparently had no intention of living the life of a wild bear.

Grandfather Mountain Resort is located in northwest North Carolina, about 90 miles west of Winston-Salem. Indians named the area Tanawha, meaning "a fabulous hawk or eagle." Early pioneers recognized the profile of an old man in the mountain's ridgeline and gave it the popular name of today. It is now one of North Carolina's top scenic attractions.

Mildred had come to Grandfather Mountain from the Atlanta Zoo, where she had been a favorite pet of the zoo office since shortly after her birth. So when she was first brought to Grandfather Mountain, she would hang around the snack bar, pester tourists for handouts, and even follow visitors home to the nearby towns and villages. Predictably, a full grown black bear — all six feet and 400 pounds — in a small North Carolina community created quite a commotion. Finally, the staff at Grandfather Mountain decided to rectify the situation. Mildred was brought deep within the park to a special habitat built just for her, where she could dwell happily (and be properly supervised). Mildred was so tame that the Grandfather Mountain staff allowed her to come and go at will, without incident, among the tourists.

Time went by, and nature took its course, and twins were born to Mildred in 1969. Their names were Maxi and Mini. Soon, a third most unusual characteristic in Mildred was revealed. Most mother bears are extremely protective of their cubs and pose a serious threat to anyone foolish enough to come between them. But Mildred showed great tolerance of the attention that the staff showered upon the cubs — much to the surprise of all who witnessed. In 1970, Mildred gave birth a second time, to a cub named Honey.

Soon afterwards another cub, whose mother was not Mildred, came to live in Mildred's habitat. His name was Hobo. Hobo become a sort of ambassador of good will for the North Carolina State Zoo, and for a bond issue affecting the financing of the zoo. Hobo traveled all about the state, making appearances on television shows and in newspaper offices on behalf of the bond campaign. Mildred, in her typical mild-mannered way, took Hobo's comings and goings very much in stride. Hobo eventually grew up in Mildred's habitat and became father to several cubs.

In 1971, Mildred birthed two more cubs. A third cub, an orphan named Punkin, was brought to Grandfather Mountain to be raised by Mildred. In the wild, bears will often reject orphaned cubs of other litters, but not Mildred. Punkin's mother had died before Punkin's eyes had opened (which usually doesn't happen until the cub is 40 days old). This seemed to aid the adoption further, as Punkin seemed to fit into the family easily. In all, Mildred gave birth to ten cubs, and "adopted" three.

As the years went by, Mildred became a folk hero around Grandfather Mountain. The bear habitat that had been constructed for her was named the Mildred the Bear Environmental Habitat. All of her cubs have grown to maturity, and Mini, Maxi, and Mildred have all been immortalized in paintings and sculptures. One of the most photographed bears in the world, Mildred has appeared on television, on postcards, in murals, in magazines, and in books.

Black bears do well to live to five years of age in the wild. Mildred, in her usual unusualness, lived to the grand old age of 26. She died on January 1, 1993. The Associated Press transmitted the story throughout the United States, and immediately cards and telegrams arrived by the score, mostly from former children who had come to Grandfather Mountain and had been captivated by this unusually peaceful, charming bear. Mildred was buried in an animal cemetery on Grandfather Mountain, on a site which had once been an orchard for early settlers of northwest North Carolina. A most unusual final resting place, for a most unusual bear.

SOURCE: Morton, Hugh. *Mildred the Bear.* Published by the author, 1993.

ANIMAL: George
DOB: Probably 1961
DOD: April 26, 1989
DESCRIPTION: Burmese python (*Python molurus bivittatus*), 16' long, 120 pounds.

Master Sergeant Dewey C. Simpson commanded a special force of CIDGs (Civilian Irregular Defense Groups) while stationed near Chau Lang in the Tri Ton District of An Gang province, in the Mekong Delta south of Saigon, near the Cambodian border of South Vietnam. The CIDGs were Cambodian men, trained and paid by the United States government to assist in fighting the Vietnam War. The special force was camped in an occupied rice paddy, slightly smaller than a city block, in the area known as the Seven Mountains.

While away from camp in August of 1963, Simpson and several of his men spotted a 10-foot Burmese python slithering across the earth. The Cambodians became quite excited, for in Cambodia python is considered as much of a delicacy as lobster is in the United States. But instead of allowing it to become supper, Simpson decided the python should become the camp's mascot. The snake was named George because, according to Chester A. Townsend, the soldier credited with naming the python, "That's what his name is!" A cage of wire and teakwood was constructed for George, who was probably three to five years old at the time. On the cage was a sign saying:

> My Name is George.
> Rules: Do not kick at George.
> Do not put more than one rat in George's cage at a time.
> Do not spit on George.

Rats, chickens, and rabbits caught in the brush were provided for George's meals. George quickly became a celebrity of the camp and was occasionally allowed to crawl about the grounds free from his cage.

On November 26, 1963, George was wounded during a mortar attack. The python was struck by shrapnel on the left side of his body, at about the middle of his length. George was quickly bandaged by a medic, and the wound healed completely, leaving only a small scar.

Soon afterwards, Sgt. Simpson received orders to return to the United States. Knowing pythons like to sleep after a big meal, Simpson fed George five chickens in preparation for the flight home. No one was interested having a hungry ten-foot python trapped in a crowded transport plane 30,000 feet above the ground.

GEORGE
(photo by "John Rottet, courtesy of the Raleigh Times." Photo was published
in Mary Ann Brittain's *A Snake Called George* and is used with permission
from the North Carolina State Museum of Natural Sciences)

After several bouts with nervous customs and agricultural inspectors, Simpson and George finally arrived in the United States. After considering several options for George's permanent home, including the Chicago Zoo and Grant's Park Zoo in Atlanta, Simpson decided to give George to the North Carolina State Museum of Natural Sciences. The python arrived February 5, 1964.

At first, George did not take to his new home. He would not eat and he was beginning to appear sick. Finally, museum officials contacted Sgt. Simpson, who had been shipped to an assignment in Panama. Simpson advised them to bathe George in warm water. When they did, George passed a large colony of tapeworms into the water. The python recovered almost immediately, and lived a healthy life in his original museum cage for 13 more years.

Burmese pythons are found near rivers and streams throughout Southeast Asia. Among the largest serpents in the world, they can reach a length of 20 feet and weigh more than 250 pounds. Unlike boas, which bear live young, pythons lay eggs, which hatch in about three months. Burmese pythons eat anything from rodents, birds, and bats to monitor lizards and even small deer. They capture their prey by means of constriction, which does not crush the animal, but merely suffocates it. The prey is swallowed whole, and if the meal is large enough, the snake may not eat again for several days.

By 1977, George had grown to most of his 16-foot length, and he weighed more than 120 pounds. Far too large for his old cage, George moved into a thermostatically controlled, hexagonal glass enclosure. Visitors to the Museum of Natural History could easily view George climbing, crawling, and eating in his comfortable, ultra-modern quarters. And there were lots of visitors — thousands, as a matter of fact. For George had become, by far, the museum's most popular attraction. On September 22, 1985, 7,000 visitors waited in the rain to watch George outside the museum in a portable cage and to listen to Sgt. Simpson tell of the python's life in Vietnam. Thousands of children had grown up with George; many had George T-shirts; and each February, in an annual ritual, children from all over North Carolina sent valentines to George.

By 1989, at 28 years of age, George had contracted glandular cancer of the jaw. His weight quickly fell to 100 pounds, and he could no longer feed himself. On April 26, 1989, George was transferred to the National Museum of Natural History (of the Smithsonian Institution) and put to sleep. George's body was kept for the study of cancer in reptiles.

Of all the valentines written to George over the years, one seemed to summarize the feelings of all that had seen him. "Python," it read, "you have slithered into my heart!"

SOURCES: Brittain, Mary Ann. *A Snake Called George*. Raleigh: North Carolina State Museum of Natural Sciences, 1987. / Quillan, Martha. "George the Python Dies at 28." *The Raleigh News and Observer*, April 28, 1989. P. 1A.

North Dakota

ANIMAL: Clyde
DOB: January 1965
DOD: June 4, 1987
DESCRIPTION: Kodiak bear (*Ursus arctos*), 9' tall, approximately 2000 pounds, brown coat.

The Kodiak brown bear is a formidable creature, the largest carnivore in North America. Actually, the Kodiak bear is the same species as the grizzly bear, but in Alaska they seem to grow even larger than those in the other states and Canada. In any case, a very large specimen — reputed to be the largest ever held in captivity — enthralled the residents of Bismarck and the rest of North Dakota for almost 20 years. He was known as the Lord of Dakota Zoo.

His name was Clyde. He stood more than nine feet tall and weighed more than 2000 pounds. He arrived as a small cub from Kodiak Island, Alaska, in 1965, weighing at that time a mere 196 pounds. He had originally been a research animal for the federal government in Alaska. Dakota Zoo worker Jerry Landgrebe was the first to call him Clyde. "I don't know," said Landgrebe. "He just looks like a Clyde."

CLYDE
(courtesy of Dakota Zoo)

From the outset, Clyde quickly became the favorite attraction at the zoo. He could occasionally be moody and grouchy, sometimes refusing to emerge from his enclosure. People would call to him, begging him to show himself, trying to lure him out with food. On those days he wouldn't budge, and nobody would dare budge him. But most days he would be playful and demonstrative, raising his massive frame to its full height, drawing gasps of amazement from the adoring throngs. He would playfully splash water at startled visitors, and his good-natured gentleness endeared him to children, who would stare at him with sparkling eyes and open mouths. He regularly ate 20 pounds of food each day, a varied menu that included lettuce trimmings, bread crusts, prepared dog food, and — as a special treat — fish. He had a special affinity for Orange Crush and jelly donuts.

By 1973, Clyde had outgrown his first cage. Moving him to his new facility required the combined efforts of ten men, with five shots of tranquilizer, a wire mesh stretcher, and a tractor.

In his new, larger cage, Clyde was provided a roommate — a female Kodiak brown bear named Bonnie. Zoo officials hoped that nature would take its course, and cubs would soon come along. But unfortunately, Bonnie and Clyde did not hit it off. "Clyde was a bachelor too long," said zoo founder Marc Christianson. The two seemed, at best, to simply tolerate each other; in truth, they did not get along too well, and eventually it became obvious that cubs would be out of the question.

Nevertheless, Clyde became an institution within an institution, and a landmark attraction in to Bismarck. Thousands came to visit him during his 20-year reign as Lord of Dakota Zoo. His gargantuan frame had been featured in the local newspaper, and his great, gentle muzzle had graced the front page of both the local phone book and the city map.

Finally, at the age of 22, the old bear died on June 4, 1987, at 9:00 P.M. Zoo workers had found Clyde lying on his side at about 4:00 P.M., breathing heavily and unable to get up. The zoo director found him still alive at 6:30, but by 9:00 he was dead. He had died of old age, a general breakdown of tissues. Although Alaskan brown bears can reach an age of 30 years, Clyde was considered an old bear, especially given his tremendous size.

The zoo board quickly decided to have Clyde stuffed and mounted, and displayed at the Dakota Zoo as a reminder of the joy and entertainment he provided visitors over the years. The public outpouring at his death provided the impetus for a fundraising campaign for the redevelopment of the Dakota Zoo. This redevelopment led in particular to the construction of the new Bear Habitat, a naturalistic enclosure for the bears which includes grass, trees, a hill, a stream, and plenty of room for the bears to roam. At the ripe old age of 23, Bonnie — Clyde's co-habitor and would-be companion — continues to thrive in the habitat inspired by Clyde.

SOURCES: "Clyde, Our Giant Bear, Dead at 22." *The Bismarck Tribune*, June 5, 1987. P. 1A. / "Clyde Will Be Stuffed, Mounted." *The Bismarck Tribune*, June 6, 1987. P. 1A. / "Clyde Made Many Friends around N.D." *The Bismarck Tribune*, June 7, 1987. / "The Bear Facts." Dakota Zoo, 1986. P. 13.

Ohio

ANIMAL: Martha
DOB: 1885
DOD: September 1914
DESCRIPTION: Passenger pigeon (*Ectopistes migratorius*), 16" tall; blue head, nape, wings, tail; peach-colored breast, throat; black bill, red eyes, orange feet.

She stood about 16 inches tall, adorned in plumage of sky-blue and peach. Her bright red eyes shone alertly. One hundred and fifty years ago, she would have gone unnoticed among the billions of her race. But by August 1910, she stood alone as a monument to human ignorance, and as the clearest testament yet to the manner in which the human race paves a path toward extinction. Eighty years later, her spectre reminds us of the effect humans can have on the rest of creation. Her name was Martha. She was the last passenger pigeon.

Martha was the last of a species so numerous and so gregarious that its members would travel in flocks numbering 2000 million birds at a time. Such a flock would float across the sky like some great storm cloud, blocking out the sun with the density of its numbers. Such a cloud would "rain" excrement upon the land. The pigeons, roosting in such great numbers, were known to pull large branches and small trees down to the ground with the weight of the birds.

The passenger pigeon's great numbers apparently did not start to diminish appreciatively until the seventeenth century. The race had managed to survive among the nature and native peoples of North America for at least 4000 years. Yet Europeans, who had witnessed the flight of the passenger pigeon for the first time in 1534, managed to wipe out the entire species in less than four centuries. Though direct hunting and destruction of habitat do not entirely account for the species' demise, there is no doubt that these factors substantially contributed to its fate.

Hunting took a heavy toll. So incredibly numerous did the passenger pigeon seem in eighteenth and nineteenth century America that hunters surely felt they could catch and kill the pigeons forever. Squabs provided a tasty treat, and great numbers of them fetched a fine price: One man made more than $60,000 in less than two weeks.

The hunters' greed for these birds became manifest in their hunting techniques. One such technique was called "stool-pigeoning." It involved capturing a live pigeon and, in some untenable manner, sewing its eyes shut. The "hunter" would then bait the ground with grain or salt, and rig a large net over the area, which would be sprung by the trapper when enough birds were attracted by the thrashing "stool-pigeon." As many as 1300 birds have been caught in one such attempt; 24,000 in ten days.

Pigeons were caught when trappers would fell trees covered with roosting birds. Hunters would suffocate them by burning grass surrounding the flocks. They would even intoxicate them, lacing seeds with alcohol; after the birds gobbled the seeds, trappers would simply collect the drunken pigeons by hand. Some trappers would simply knock the birds from a tree or a post with a pole. By the mid–1800s, passenger pigeon numbers were in decline. Protective measures were enacted in a number of states to curb the activities of trappers but because they were largely unenforced, they were mostly ineffective. In addition to hunting, development of land continued throughout the nation, which contributed heavily to destruction of nesting areas for all animals, including the passenger pigeon.

The ultimate demise of the passenger pigeon advanced rapidly. The last large nesting area in New England was observed in Massachusetts in 1851; the last Massachusetts nest, in the 1880s; and the last New England record of any kind, in 1894. The pigeons quickly disappeared from the Eastern Seaboard, the east-central states, and finally the Great Lakes. Michigan housed the last refuge for the passenger pigeon, with the last nest spotted in 1886. The last undisputed sighting of any wild passenger pigeon was recorded in 1896.

While the pigeons marched towards extinction in the wild, several conservation groups set up captive breeding programs in the faint hope of saving the species. One such collection was kept in Chicago by C.O. Whitman, a pioneer in the science of animal behavior. Unfortunately, the inbreeding from such programs produced infertile eggs, and the few pigeons left continued to die off.

By 1908, the total world population — held by Whitman — was eight; one of these birds was transferred to the Cincinnati Zoo. Its name was Martha, named for George Washington's wife. By 1910, Martha was the only passenger pigeon left in the world. On a September morning in 1914, Martha was found dead in her cage. She was frozen in a cake of ice and sent to the Smithsonian to be preserved. Remarkably, she was 29 years old when she died.

SOURCES: Halliday, Tim. *Vanishing Birds.* New York: Holt, Rinehart, and Winston, 1978. Pp. 87–94. / Edey, Maitland. "Once There Were Billions." *Marvels and Mysteries of Our Animal World.* Pleasantville, N.Y.: Reader's Digest Association, 1964.

Oklahoma

ANIMAL: Snoopy
DOB: 1965
DOD: Presumably early 1980s
DESCRIPTION: Persian and angora cat, white, three marks behind right shoulder blade.

The candidate for the most famous beast in the history of Oklahoma is named Snoopy. It is not a dog, and it has nothing to do with the Red Baron. This story is even more unbelievable.

In October 1970, Garrett Cook, Sr., his wife, and his 17-year-old son, Tim, moved from Duke, Oklahoma (about 60 miles south of Elk City) to Chickasha (about 35 miles southwest of Oklahoma City), a total of nearly 110 miles. When they arrived at their new home, they found that Snoopy, their white Persian and angora mixed cat, had disappeared. Apparently the cat had ambled away from the family car at a convenience stop on the way to Chickasha.

Over the next several weeks, Garrett Cook, Sr., and his family ran several ads in the local Chickasha newspaper, searching for their beloved feline. But the ads proved futile. Then something amazing happened.

In February 1971, the family of Garrett Cook, Jr., was relaxing at their home in Oilsdale, California. Suddenly five-year-old Dennis shouted, "Snoopy's back!" Mrs. Cook opened the front door, and into the house ran the long-missing cat. Snoopy raced directly for his old favorite spot under the ironing board near the dining room.

Two years previously, the families of Garrett Cook, Sr., and Garrett Cook, Jr., had lived in the same house in Oilsdale, just north of Bakersfield, California. Mrs. Cook, Sr., had given the cat to her son Tim while they all lived in Oilsdale, where they had lived for 20 years. The family surmised that when Snoopy wandered off en route to Chickasha, he somehow instinctively headed for his original home to find Tim. Garrett, Jr., explained, "There was a bond between the cat and my brother [Tim] you couldn't explain ... he was like a shadow."

The Cooks had no explanation as to how Snoopy could have possibly survived a 1500-mile hike from Oklahoma to California. On the other hand, a cat is a cat, and it has 40 million years of survival instinct from which to draw. Snoopy probably fended for himself the way his species has always done. "He might have gotten a ride part of the way or something," added Mrs. Cook.

The fact that the story seemed unbelievable was not lost on several members of the local media. Not only did all accounts of the event originate from within the same family and apart from objective witnesses, but the sequence of events was remarkably similar to 1951 incident involving a cream-colored Persian cat named Sugar.

In that story, the Woods family had moved from California to Oklahoma, leaving Sugar with the new owners of the California house. Fourteen months later Sugar was found in an Oklahoma barn at the Woods' new home. Dr. J.B. Rhine of Duke University published a paper in the *Journal of Parapsychology* in 1962 concerning the Sugar episode. He used Sugar's 1500-mile journey as an example of Psi-trailing, a method utilized by animals to track a companion without any obvious sensory trail.

The Cooks staunchly claim that the cat who showed up at their doorstep was indeed Snoopy — not some imposter, as had been suggested — and cited three phenomena as evidence:

1. The family of Garrett, Jr., identified the cat that walked into their house as Snoopy because of the three marks behind his right shoulder blade.

2. Snoopy appeared at the Oilsdale doorstep frayed and tattered from the long trip. His paws were red and raw, his claws worn to the nubs, his body tired and thin, and his fur matted and filthy.

3. The family dog, Baron, who normally would have nothing whatsoever to do with cats, took to the prodigal cat right away, just as it had to Snoopy.

In any case, Tim Cook and Snoopy were reunited in Chickasha, Oklahoma, in March of 1971. The Cooks had a family reunion that none of them would soon forget.

SOURCES: "All's Well — Cat Finds Old Home." *The Daily Oklahoman*, February 2, 1971. / Tremain, Ruthven. *The Animals' Who's Who.* New York: Charles Scribner's Sons, 1982. P. 246.

Oregon

ANIMAL: Scannon
DOB: Probably around 1799
DOD: Probably around 1812
DESCRIPTION: Newfoundland dog, black, shaggy coat, 27" at shoulder, 147 pounds.

The characters and personalities who comprised the Lewis and Clark Expedition in 1803 have added to the mystique that surrounds this amazing nineteenth-century adventure. The extraordinary people who joined the expedition included:

Captain Meriwether Lewis (1774–1809) — Thomas Jefferson's private secretary, a veteran of the army, and a fellow Virginian, who was chosen by Jefferson to lead the expedition. Lewis committed suicide in 1809.

Captain William Clark (1770–1838) — Invited by a letter from Meriwether Lewis to co-lead the adventure. Clark was a longtime veteran of the Indian Wars.

Sergeant George Drouillard (unknown) — French Canadian expert in sign language, which all the Plains Indians understood. He joined the expedition on November 11, 1803.

Sacagawea, the Bird Woman (1784–1884) — The legendary Shoshone Indian woman who helped the expedition survive the wilderness by bargaining with local tribes for horses and other supplies. She, along with husband and French-Canadian trapper Toussaint Charbonneau, acted as guide for much of the expedition.

Sergeant Patrick Gass (1771–1870) — Indian fighter, veteran soldier, boat builder, carpenter, he helped build Fort Clatsop on the Pacific Coast of Oregon. Gass went on to publish a book about the journey called the *Journal of the Lewis and Clark Expedition*.

Of all those who made the trek, probably the least known is a black Newfoundland dog owned by Meriwether Lewis. In fact, something of a controversy has arisen over the actual name of this Newfoundland. The discrepancy seems to have been produced by a combination of penmanship and the effect of time on ink. Apparently the dog's name has varied according to which authentic, handwritten journal from the expedition a particular historian has consulted. These journals have referred to the dog as Scannon, Seamon, Semon, Scamon, Scammon, and Seman, and the differences may well be due to the degree of disintegration the particular inked script has experienced. In any case, this Newfoundland joined in the adventures with the rest of the party and, in its own way, contributed to the success and fame of the mission.

The Louisiana Purchase in 1803 was the door for westward expansion of

A SCANNON FACSIMILE
(courtesy of Lewis & Clark Heritage Foundation)

the United States. Needing cash for troops and supplies for his wars in Europe, Napoleon Bonaparte shortsightedly agreed to sell all of the lands of the Louisiana Territory to Thomas Jefferson and the fledgling United States. This included a vast amount of territory west of the Mississippi River. At the purchase price of $15,000,000, this amounted to a per-acre price of about four cents.

To fully examine what he had purchased, Thomas Jefferson obtained $2500 from Congress, and selected Meriwether Lewis to head the examination. Lewis, in turn, selected Clark as co-leader, and together with about 40 soldiers and civilians, three boats, a keelboat, and two dugout canoes, they set out to explore the land obtained by the Louisiana Purchase.

The adventure actually began on August 30, 1803, when Lewis left Pittsburgh, Pennsylvania. He met up with Clark in St. Louis on March 30, 1804, and the Lewis and Clark trail went on to wind its way along the Missouri River through what are now the states of Missouri, Nebraska, South Dakota, North Dakota, Montana, Idaho, and Oregon. In Oregon, under the direction of carpenter Patrick Gass, they built Fort Clatsop in what is now Astoria, Oregon. After spending the winter in Oregon, the party returned east. Splitting into two groups to explore the Rockies, they reunited at Fort Union in North Dakota. The explorers returned to St. Louis on September 23, 1806. Amazingly, only one individual died during the entire three-year expedition — apparently of appendicitis.

Meriwether Lewis had purchased the dog, whom we shall call Scannon, in Ohio for $20, a substantial price in 1803. Once, outside of Cairo, Illinois, a Shawnee Indian offered three beaverskins for the black Newfoundland, but Lewis turned him down. Scannon was a loyal dog of gentle temperament, and he accompanied Lewis through the whole of the journey.

The origin of the Newfoundland breed may be based on white Great Pyrenees, brought to the coast of Newfoundland by Basque fishermen. Others believe it is descended from the French hound. In any case, it originated in Newfoundland, where the dogs would need thick coats, as well as excellent swimming ability. Many a Newfoundland has rescued a human sailor or swimmer from a watery grave off the east coast of Canada.

Scannon's most important moment of the expedition came on May 29, 1805, outside Fort Manden in North Dakota. The party had camped for the night on the western bank of the Missouri River. Scannon slept outside Lewis' tent, as was his custom. All was quiet in the night, when suddenly a noise like thunder erupted from the bank of the river. A bull American bison, having swum easily across the river, had not noticed the party's boats moored up on the eastern shore. The buffalo apparently stepped into one of the boats and tripped, and in a frightened rage, it stormed headlong into the camp. The bison's direction would have led it directly into the tents of several of the party, who no doubt would have been killed or badly injured by 1600 pounds of fury. Fortunately, Scannon awoke immediately and charged toward the buffalo. The Newfoundland's barking scared the bison into changing direction, saving the men from being trampled to death. One account of the incident claimed that the beast had stampeded through the camp, "just missing by inches the heads of a group of sleeping men."

Scannon functioned as a valuable retriever on the many hunts that provided much of the party's sustenance. Geese and ducks of many varieties were gathered for the hunters by the Newfoundland. In several instances Scannon provided the meal himself, catching squirrels for supper as the rodents swam across a nearby river.

Scannon also suffered his share of hardships during the trip. Mosquitoes seemed particularly attracted to him, especially along the Missouri River, and he would howl in torment at the biting insects. In Montana Scannon was bitten by a beaver, and in Oregon he was stolen (and later returned) by local natives. Despite such misadventures, Scannon managed to return with Lewis to St. Louis, completing the Lewis and Clark Expedition. This expedition, whose discoveries were well chronicled in several journals, was the key that opened the door provided by the Louisiana Purchase and allowed the western expansion of the United States.

The last record of Scannon appears in the journal of Meriwether Lewis on July 15, 1806. Lewis writes, "My dog...howls with the torture he experiences from [mosquitoes]." Nothing more is known about the dog. Some have surmised that he inadvertently was left behind in the wilds of Montana on a later excursion by Lewis. Others suggest that he may have been killed by a grizzly bear. On the other hand, there is no good reason to believe Scannon did not live a long life at the side of his legendary master. After all, if the Newfoundland could survive the Lewis and Clark Expedition, he could likely survive just about anything.

SOURCES: Jackson, Donald, and Osgood, Ernest S. *The Lewis and Clark Expedition's Newfoundland Dog*. Great Falls, Mont.: Lewis and Clark Trail Heritage Foundation, 1990. / Quaife, Milo M. *The Journals of Captain Meriwether Lewis and Sergent John Ordway*. Madison, Wis.: State Historical Society, 1916.

Pennsylvania

ANIMAL: Punxsutawney Phil
DOB: 1886
DOD: Still alive, if you believe the Chamber of Commerce
DESCRIPTION: Groundhog (*Marmota monax*), 26" long, 14 pounds, brownish-grey coat.

As the legend tells it, on February 2, the groundhog pokes his head out of his den and takes a good look around. If he happens to see his shadow on the ground before him, it means six more weeks of winter. If he doesn't, good news! Spring is on its way! The question is, in North America, which groundhog do you believe? Among the wondrous woodchuck contenders are included such prodigious prognosticators as:

— Jimmy V. from Sun Prairie, Wisconsin
— Melvin from Greensboro, North Carolina
— Octorara Orphie from Quarryville, Pennsylvania
— French Creek Freddie from West Virginia
— Buckeye Chuck from Marion, Ohio
— Dave from Dunkirk, New York
— Tilly from Tacoma, Washington
— Willie from Ontario
— Woodrow K. Woodchuck from West Orange, New Jersey

Without a doubt, however, the most famous groundhog of all is Punxsutawney Phil, from the western Pennsylvania town of Punxsutawney, some 75 miles northeast of Pittsburgh. Ambassadors of Punxsutawney Phil's Groundhog Club come from as far away as Canada, South America, and Europe.

Phil's fame was further enchanced by the release of the 1991 Paramount

PUNXSUTAWNEY PHIL
(courtesy of Punxsutawney Ground Hog Club)

movie *Groundhog Day*, starring Bill Murray, Andie MacDowell and Phil. *Groundhog Day* told the story of a prima donna weatherman (Murray's character, also named Phil) from Pittsburgh, sent for the fourth year in a row to cover the Groundhog Day festival in Punxsutawney — an assignment he has snobbishly loathed each year. And, through the magic of the movies, the weatherman is forced to live the same day — Groundhog Day in Punxsutawney - over and over again, until he learns to appreciate the people, the event and the town itself.

The legend of the groundhog may have originated in connection with the Christian Feast of Candlemas, which also falls on February 2. Candlemas, according to church tradition, celebrates the presentation and purification of the Christ Child at the Jewish temple by the Virgin Mary. In old English tradition, the weather of Candlemas was used as a foretelling of the coming of spring. If Candlemas was sunny, winter would continue; if it was cloudy and rainy, spring was about to begin.

The groundhog, or woodchuck, is a rodent common throughout the country. They usually grow to be about two feet long and weigh about 14 pounds. Besides their climatic insight, their greatest claim to fame — or infamy — is the holes with which they perforate the gardens, lawns, and backyards of North America. On February 2, the groundhog is a hero; for most of the rest of the year, he's a flat-out nuisance.

Punxsutawney, a small coal-mining and manufacturing town with a population of 6782, was settled in 1814. Its name comes from the Indian word Ponkuttenick, meaning "Gnat-Town." Phil is its leading celebrity and the centerpiece of its tourist industry. Each February 2 since 1887, local residents and far-flung visitors have gathered at Gobbler's Knob, where they witness the weathercasting by Punxsutawney Phil. Flanked by the "Inner Circle of the

Groundhog Club"— all well versed in "Groundhogese"— the president of the club interprets Phil's forecast for the multitudes, and the festivities begin. The day's events include a community breakfast, the selection of a Groundhog King and Queen, and an evening banquet hosted by the Inner Circle. The following weeks feature a stream of parades, hobby shows, stage productions, dances, contests, sidewalk sales, and more in honor of the "Seer of Seers."

Apparently unaffected by it all, Phil resides with his family in a climate-controlled, simulated burrow in the Civic Building at the Groundhog Zoo next to the Punxsutawney Library. Each February 1, Phil is transferred from his home at the zoo to his tree stump at Gobbler's Knob. The local National Guard stands watch over him to ensure, as the locals say, that he "will be safe and is able to meditate on his very important prediction." And though the average life span for an ordinary groundhog is 12 years, a Punxsutawney Chamber of Commerce spokesperson stands by the claim that Phil's age is 108 years.

As for the veracity of Phil's predictions, Punxsutawney residents swear by them: "All of the news people, all of the TV people are here in Punxy," says Bill Null of the Punxsutawney Chamber of Commerce. "Our prediction is entered into the Congressional Record every year."

Of course, supernatural accuracy is claimed for all of the other *Marmota* meteorologists as well. But for most of the movie-going American public — and certainly for the residents of western Pennsylvania — Groundhog Day happens in Punxsutawney. "When florists are sending orders to Groundhogsville," said Null, "they're not sending them to Sun Prairie."

SOURCES: Selby, Gardner. "Jimmy V. Predicts Spring's Nearly Here!" *Capital Times* (Sun Prarie, Wisconsin), February 2, 1987. Punxsutawney Chamber of Commerce.

Puerto Rico

ANIMAL: Moises
DOB: October 1991
DESCRIPTION: Manatee (*Trichecus manatus*), 15' long, 3500 pounds, gray, hairless hide.

On November 4, 1991, a city painter was working on the Avenue Los Dominicos Bridge, which crosses one of the channels in Levittown, Toa Baja, Puerto Rico. Pausing momentarily from his labors, the painter glanced downward toward the placid water. Suddenly he spotted a dark gray object floating on the surface. As he watched more closely, he determined the object was an animal, and it was alive, though barely.

The painter left his station and called the police, who in turn alerted the Caribbean Stranding Network (CSN). The CSN is a network of more than 60 Caribbean organizations — including Red Caribena de Varamientos of San Juan — dedicated to the rescue and rehabilitation of animals within the Caribbean Islands. The CSN coordinated the rescue with local staff and volunteers, and the animal — a very sick and weak baby manatee, whose mother was nowhere to be found — was transported to the Laboratorios Marinos de Isla Magueyes in La Parguera, Lajas, on the southwest corner of Puerto Rico.

At La Parguera, the task of rehabilitation began. It was determined that the manatee was about two weeks old, and weakened in part because it had not nursed in many days. Although the mother was never found, many believed that the animal had been poached, its meat likely sold illegally. It was also discovered that the manatee had ingested a plastic bag, which had probably been dumped into the channel. Plastic bags and plastic beverage can holders are a terrible threat to marine mammals, who swallow them, and waterbirds, who become tangled and strangled in the plastic circles. Every year, thousands of animals are injured and killed by these insidious forms of pollution.

The rehabilitation team started raising the young manatee on a milk diet, which eventually was expanded to lettuce, carrots, apples and bananas. Meanwhile, the manatee attracted the attention of media and well-wishers throughout the Island of Puerto Rico. A contest was conducted to name the manatee, and the name Moises, which means "Rescued from the Waters," was chosen.

Manatees are found throughout the Caribbean, but in numbers much diminished from the original population. While water pollution has contributed greatly to their demise, the slow-swimming manatees are particularly vulnerable to collisions with power boats and jet ski equipment. Steel propellers from these craft can inflict serious wounds upon the harmless, slow-moving animals. In Puerto Rico, it is estimated there are between 60 and 250 manatees, the majority of which live on the southern and eastern coasts. Because of their small numbers, these timid creatures are often very difficult to spot. Moises, therefore, provided a unique opportunity for the people of Puerto Rico to study this unusual animal up close.

The mammalian order Sirenia is comprised of the manatee (*Trichecus manatus*) and its cousin the Dugong (*Dugong dugon*). A third sirenian, the huge Steller's Sea Cow (*Hydrodamalis stelleri*), was overhunted into extinction by 1768. The manatee can grow from three feet long (Moises' length at rescue) and 80 pounds to more than 15 feet and 3500 pounds. Its body is shaped like that of a pinniped, except that its forelimbs are flippers, and instead of hindlimbs it has a solid, muscular, oar-shaped tail. Its bulbous and whiskered face resembles that of an ash-colored walrus without tusks. A gentle, quiet creature, the manatee fees on soft aquatic vegetation growing at the bottom of the estuaries and seas in which it lives.

As the months passed, Moises grew healthier and larger, and within two years he had reached well over 600 pounds. He became a national celebrity, the symbol of the environmental movement and the CSN in Puerto Rico. He drew hundreds of visitors from all over the island, many of whom came bearing heads of lettuce. Moises inspired local interest in the endangered status of manatees in particular, and of marine wildlife in general.

At 30 months, Moises was transferred to a marine rehabilitation center, where he would learn to adapt to a marine environment. He was gently weaned off lettuce and onto aquatic plants, and he grew less and less dependent upon his human benefactors. After five months, in the fall of 1994, Moises was released to the wild, carrying a transmitter so that his position could be followed. All reports indicate that he is healthy, and his assimilation into his marine home has been a success.

SOURCES: Darling, Kathy. *Manatee on Location*. New York: Lothrop, Lee, and Shepard, 1991. / "Moises." Red Caribena Varamientos. March 21, 1994, Lajas, PR.

Rhode Island

ANIMAL: The Chepachet Elephant
DOB: 1810
DOD: July 31, 1822
DESCRIPTION: Asiatic elephant (*Elephas maximus*), 7' 6" at shoulder, 6000 pounds.

The early 1800s was an age of discovery for the fledgling United States. As it sought to expand its national borders on the North American continent, the country strove to extend its understanding and influence abroad. The new products, customs, peoples, and animals discovered and brought home during the expansion were met with simultaneous reactions of surprise, doubt, wonder, and fear.

Chepachet, ten miles northwest of Providence, was the center for commercial, agricultural, and business enterprise in the northern part of Rhode Island in those days. Honest merchants and charlatans alike brought wares and wiles from all over the world to entertain the local population. Common entertainments included wild animal exhibits, in which showmen would present fabulous creatures from the four corners of the globe to stir the local imaginations, anxieties, and pocketbooks. At that time, species from other lands — even those that now seem ordinary to anyone with a television — were objects of great mystery and astonishment.

In 1822, a most enterprising "amusement manager" brought a special exhibit to the town of Chepachet. Billboards posted throughout the town promised:

An Exhibition of a Natural Curiosity
    The Learned Elephant
which for sagacity and docility, exceeds any one ever imported into this county
will go through her astonishing performances which have excited the admira-
tion of every beholder...

The exhibition promised a female, 12-year-old elephant, six and one-half
feet high, 19 feet long, weighing between five and six thousand pounds. The
billboards further advertised the amazing feats the animal would perform,
describing the manner in which it would eat and drink with its trunk. The
animal's proud owner even proclaimed its hide so thick that no bullet could
ever penetrate it. This final boast proved to be the owner's undoing.

On July 31, 1822, hundreds of Rhode Islanders flocked to the grounds of
Cyrus Cooke's Inn in Chepachet to view the amazing beast, paying 12 cents
for adults, six cents for children. The spectators were invited to touch, pet,
and in some cases, even ride the marvelous creature. The owner gave a lecture
on the peculiarities of the elephant, which demonstrated the use of its trunk
in many capacities. The audience marveled as the elephant kneeled, sat, lay
down, and moved about at the commands of the owner. And at each performance, the manager particularly emphasized the special properties of the hide,
explaining that since the elephant could not be felled by a bullet because of
its skin, it was all but impossible to kill.

By the end of the last performance, evening had fallen, and the tents that
held the exhibition were razed. Appreciative members of the day's largest audience lingered behind to congratulate the showman and to shower praise on
his show and his elephant. Finally, at about midnight, the elephant was led
away.

In order to reach the night's lodging, the elephant and his trainer had to
walk from the inn to the Chepachet Creek, cross the wooden bridge spanning
the creek, and pass an old grist mill by which stood an ancient elm tree. The
moon cast bright, silvery light and eery shadows as the elephant stepped care-
fully upon the little bridge. Suddenly, a gunshot rang out from the direction
of the old grist mill. The bullet pierced the elephant's brain through its right
eye, and the great beast dropped like a felled oak.

A posse of sorts was hastily assembled, and its search quickly apprehended
five local boys, who apparently had been unable to take the boasts of the showman at face value. They had obtained a rifle and, from behind the elm tree at
which they were captured, had fired at the elephant.

At a highly publicized trial, all five boys were found guilty of planning
and executing the foul deed. Each was sentenced to pay his share of the resti-
tution — totaling more than $1500 — which was not collected in its entirety
until four years later.

This episode occurred many years ago, and therefore, little evidence
remains. Controversy surrounds the dispensation of the elephant's carcass. Its

hide, some say, was tanned and sent to a Boston museum. Others claim it may be buried somewhere around Chepachet. A flood of 1867 wiped out the grist mill, and the mighty elm tree was felled by a woodsman's axe. But stories are still told of the Chepachet Elephant killed by the curiosity that surrounded it.

SOURCE: "Chepachet's Elephant Shot a Century Ago." *The Providence Sunday Journal,* June 18, 1922.

South Carolina

ANIMAL: Arab
DOB: March 11, 1857
DOD: 1884
DESCRIPTION: South Carolina saddle horse (*Equus caballus*), smallish, perhaps 15 hands high; muscular grey coat.

The most famous beast of South Carolina is the only one with his own autobiography. This animal became better known for the company he kept than for the deeds he actually performed, even though his deeds were enormous in and of themselves.

In 1901, Corporal Edward Prioleau Henderson of the Hampton Legion, the Beaufort District Troop, second South Carolina Cavalry, published a book called *Autobiography of Arab*. The book, written from the point of view of Corporal Henderson's horse, Arab, details the experiences of the horse and rider under the command of Confederate general James "Jeb" Stuart during Stuart's campaigns in Maryland, Pennsylvania, and Virginia. Miraculously, Arab and his rider survived all four years of the Civil War, and quite possibly saw more of the war between the North and the South than any other horse. Arab's unique and tender point of view reminds the reader that the soldiers were not the only ones affected by the carnage and despair, the heroism and the camaraderie of those four bloody years. The animals, the civilians, even the land itself felt the irreversible effects by the bloodiest period in United States history.

The *Autobiography of Arab* begins with the horse's birth and raising on the plantation of Dr. E.R. Henderson, father of Edward Henderson, in the district of Colleton, South Carolina, west of Charleston. Arab describes his four years on the farm, where he was fed and treated well, and where he and Edward would ride and hunt foxes in the woods of South Carolina.

The narrative quickly moves into the war years, in which Henderson and Arab served among the Iron Scouts of generals Jeb Stuart and Wade Hampton. Because he was mount to the third corporal under Captain Thomas E.

AUTOBIOGRAPHY OF ARAB MARKER
(courtesy of Norman A. McCorkle, South Carolina Dept. of Archives & History)

Screven in the Beaufort District Troops, Arab's narrative provides the reader a battlefield-level view of the war. While many accounts of Civil War battles focus on the strategies and casualty figures normally considered by the generals, the horse describes the hazards, illnesses, inconveniences, and sufferings of the second South Carolina Cavalry, far from the glory and legend imparted by history.

In one moving account from the summer of 1862, Arab describes the march to Manassas, Virginia (20 miles south of Washington, D.C.), at which lay a Union supply depot. The Confederate armies of Joseph E. Johnston and Stonewall Jackson had seized the depot, and now the second South Carolina Cavalry joined those armies to confiscate food and supplies for the struggling Confederate troops. Once as many supplies as possible were loaded up, the torch was set to the rest to keep the Union from replenishing their lines at the same depot. Arab describes the scene:

> What a sight when we left there — every man's horse loaded down with things most needed. I remember, for one thing, I had a fine ham, slung on each side, and by that time of the war I had gotten very fond of bacon, for Ben (a servant) taught me to eat and drink everything that was eaten by man. I was very sorry, indeed, to see them burning up so much good corn, oats and hay, bacon, flour, etc. Many a day, in the future days of the war, when I was half starved, have I thought of the good things burnt up at the evacuation of Manassas.

The Battle of Williamsburg, Virginia, was a small, bloody portion of George B. McClellan's Peninsular Campaign in the spring of 1862. In this campaign, McClellan moved his Army of the Potomac down Chesapeake Bay and up the James and York rivers, toward the Confederate capital of Richmond, Virginia. Joseph E. Johnston's army, along with reinforcements from Stuart's cavalry, met the Army of the Potomac in the spongy, soggy mud of eastern Virginia. The result of the battle was a stalemate, with McClellan unable to advance on Richmond, and the Confederate army unable to shore up an adequate counterattack.

Arab describes how he and Corporal Henderson crossed the flood plain of the York River as they ventured to meet the enemy at Williamsburg, where part of General Stuart's army had been cut off:

> And what a crossing place it was, knee-deep in mud, and covered with dead and wounded men and horses. About the time I got there, the place was blocked on the right and left of the crossing place. The trees at each side had been cut down, to prevent crossing, except in one place. The firing at the rear at this time was getting pretty hot, for the Yankee infantry were firing on us, as well as their cavalry who were pursuing us. It seemed like there was no way of getting across except by waiting for those in front to cross over. So my master said to me, "Arab, this will never do; we must get away from here somehow, if we have to go over the fallen trees; try yourself now and take me out of this place; my life depends on your heels." He then turned me to the right, amongst the fallen trees and brush. It seemed a regular fox chase, like the old days, before the war (leaving out the bullets). I bore my rider safely to the top of the hill, where the command was reformed and the rolls called.

Similar accounts of various battles and events through the course of the war fill the pages of *The Autobiography of Arab*. Included among these are Stuart's run around McClellan, which provided invaluable information for General Lee about the Army of the Potomac, making Stuart a hero, and lifting the morale of the Confederate army; and the 96-mile march in 30 hours from Chambersburg, Pennsylvania, to Leesburg, Virginia, the entire length of which only Arab and one other horse traversed without change.

The narrative concludes after the careers of Henderson and Arab wound down in the countryside of South Carolina. Henderson married, fathered children, and moved from South Carolina to Savannah, Georgia. Arab, for his part, lived the remainder of his life in Hendersonville, on the plantation where he was raised. A state historical marker commemorating the book and its heroes now stands in Hendersonville.

In the epilogue of the book, Corporal Edward Prioleau Henderson pays loving tribute to his old, grey war-horse:

> Arab died when he was twenty-seven years old, and was decently buried "on the hill beyond the old ginhouse," on the old plantation, where he was foaled and raised. Peace to your ashes, noble horse. Your like will never be raised in Colleton County again. You loved me, and I loved and had implicit faith in you. How much so, will never be known by mortal man. Believe me, most respectfully,
>
> Arab's Master

SOURCES: Henderson, E. Prioleau. *Autobiography of Arab*. Oxford, Miss.: Guild Bindery, 1991 (reprint ed.). / Davis, William C. *The Image of War: 1861-1865. Volume II: The Guns of '62*. Gettysburg, Penn.: National Historical Society, 1982. Pp. 115, 118–119.

South Dakota

ANIMAL: Custer Wolf
DOB: Approximately 1910
DOD: October 11, 1920
DESCRIPTION: Timber wolf (*Canis lupus*), white, 6' long, 32" at shoulder,
  98 pounds.

The wolf may be the most unduly feared, most maligned creature in the
world — certainly in the United States. It is the villain in countless children's
stories and ranchers' yarns. It has been mythologized with almost human —
even superhuman — intelligence, avarice, and cruelty, and thus has earned the
nearly obsessive fear and rage of humankind.

From the outset of North American settlement, ranchers declared war on
any beast perceived as a threat to their cattle and sheep: mountain lions, bears,
bobcats, coyotes, and especially wolves. Such animals were said to have cost
millions of dollars in livestock. The nineteenth century in particular saw sense-
less massacre of thousands of wolves. Employing rifles, guns, pits, pens, cages,
steel and wooden traps, and poisons such as strychnine (inflicting a horribly
slow and painful death), bounty hunters piled up literally hundreds of wolf
carcasses, dozens often collected in a single day's spree.

By the advent of the twentieth century, *Canis lupus* was left at the door
to extinction, until bounties on wolves were brought under control by the federal government. States repealed their bounty laws, making the mass destruction of wolves illegal.

Although also known as the gray wolf, the timber wolf can be found in
shades of black, brown, silver, tan, and white. Colors are individual characteristics, and pups of varying hues can be found within the same litter — which
can number up to fourteen. The only other wolf indigenous to the United
States is the rare red wolf (*Canis rufus*) of southern Louisiana and Texas. The
red wolf regularly interbreeds with coyotes, however, and thus *Canis rufus* may
quickly be diluting itself out of existence. These wolves — along with the coy-
ote and the fox — make up the American branch of the family canidae.

While the red wolf may be hybridizing itself toward extinction, the timber wolf is endangered in a large part because of the fear it incites in ranchers. Even now, as populations of timber wolves are being reintroduced in areas
such as Yellowstone National Park, ranchers passionately express their grave
concern over the threat they feel the wolves present to their livestock. Although
pack wolves generally hunt in cooperation for large grazing animals, the diet
of the wolf can encompasses small animals including rabbits, mice, birds, and
even fish. A hungry wolf is opportunistic, however, and will eat anything it
can catch or scavenge.

For the most part, wolves and humans can coexist peacefully, provided each is given sufficient, separate territory. Wolves generally hunt wild game, such as deer or elk, in a pack of up to 20 wolves. The pack relies on coordinated hunting skills and techniques to gather its prey over an extensive hunting range, often as great as 200 square miles. Only when human development infringes upon the wolf's territory — driving off natural prey and introducing the wolf to domesticated livestock — do a rancher's cattle or sheep fall into jeopardy. Most often livestock destruction is carried out by renegade wolves who, after being isolated from the pack for some reason stumble on the simple expedient of raiding domestic stock, then continue that learned pattern.

One such specimen may be the most famous beast of South Dakota. Between 1911 and 1920, within a 60-mile range around Custer and the Black Hills of South Dakota, the ghostly white Custer Wolf destroyed more than $25,000 worth of livestock. He was known to have killed as many as 30 head of cattle in a single week. He had a reputation for cunning and cruelty; in addition to feasting on some of the finest cattle in southwest South Dakota, he became infamous for merely wounding cattle, breaking their legs, biting their tails, apparently for the savage pleasure of it. Lone ranchers out on the range shivered at the prospect of a face-to-face meeting with this marauder. Some believed his rampage was revenge for a mate that had been killed. Some believed he was part wolf, part cougar; others believed he was part wolf, part devil, charmed with a wisdom unknown among beasts. (Unfortunately, such anthropomorphic projections are common in literary depictions of the wolf; they probably tell much more of the hysteria and biases of the particular writer than of any motivation behind the wolf's behavior.)

The white wolf seemed untouchable, and a myth of invincibility developed around this animal, making it seem even more fearsome, and its destruction more imperative. Wrote naturalist and hunter Stanley Young:

> He loped through every kind of danger and spurned it all. He sniffed out the subtlest poison and passed it by. The most adroitly concealed trap was as clear to him as a mirror in the sunshine. Old hunters, unerring shots, drew the bead on him and saw him glide away unarmed. The price on his head was five hundred dollars. Bounty hunters sought him for profit. Sportsmen put forth every device to slay him for reputation's sake. And still the old wolf went unscathed about his work of destruction.

The Custer Wolf was finally tracked down in October of 1920 by H.P. Williams, a hunter sent by the U.S. Department of Agriculture to protect the livestock of the region. Williams began tracking the white wolf in March of 1920. He later told stories of how difficult it was to find the wolf, claiming coyotes acted as its bodyguards, warning it when Williams came near. Williams relayed how so often he came close to capturing the wolf, only to have it slip through his grasp moments before its intended demise. All the while, the Custer Wolf continued to kill, almost in mockery of the seemingly hapless hunter.

Finally, on the morning of October 11, the Custer Wolf stepped in a steel trap set by Williams. After dragging the trap for three miles, the wounded and beleaguered wolf was finally stopped by Williams, who shot it with his rifle. For days afterwards, telephones buzzed throughout southwest South Dakota. Ranchers and residents alike rejoiced over the news of the arch-criminal of the wild: "The Custer Wolf is dead."

SOURCES: Erskine, Laurie York. "Mighty Hunter of the Wilds." *Marvels & Mysteries of Our Animal World.* Pleasantville, N.Y.: Reader's Digest Association, 1964. Pp. 217–219. / Young, Stanley P. *The Last of the Loners.* London: Macmillan, 1970. Pp. 297–304.

Tennessee

ANIMAL: Blaze
DOB: 1943
DOD: 1945
DESCRIPTION: Bull mastiff, 30" at shoulder, 130 pounds, tawny coat.

The most famous animal of Tennessee never actually lived in the Volunteer State. In truth, he was merely a stopover. During his Christmas leave, Lt. Colonel Elliot Roosevelt, son of President Franklin Delano Roosevelt, brought a 130-pound bull mastiff named Blaze to stay at the White House. Lt. Colonel Roosevelt had purchased the dog in England. Before returning to Europe to resume his duties, he asked that Blaze be shipped out to Los Angeles to his wife, actress Faye Emerson, on the next empty bomber flying west.

Blaze was shipped from Washington, D.C., to the Air Transport Command (ATC) in Memphis, Tennessee, where his transport west would be arranged. Apparently, an unidentified staff person — either in the White House or ATC — thought it would be prudent to earn a little recognition from the Roosevelt family.

Accompanying the crate in which Blaze traveled to Memphis was an "A" priority shipping order. The "A" priority is reserved for VIPs or vitally important cargo. The shipping orders reached the ATC, and provisions were immediately made for Blaze. On January 11, 1945, in order to make room for the bull mastiff with travel priority from the White House, three servicemen — an army sergeant, a SeeBee, and a seaman first class, all bound for the West Coast — were ordered off the airplane. Their travel priorities rated only "C."

One of the stranded servicemen, heading for California on emergency leave, hitch-hiked from Memphis to Dallas, Texas. In Dallas, the serviceman lost his travel orders and was held for two days before resuming his trip to California.

A second bumped serviceman took his leave in Antioch, California, after receiving five extra days for initially being bumped from the ATC flight. Leon Leroy, an 18-year-old navy gunner, reportedly returned to his assignment at the Brooklyn Navy Yard by train. "I'm not taking any more chances," he was quoted as saying.

The fact that the president's son's dog received higher travel priority than three active servicemen was lost on neither the press nor Republican senators. Stories appeared in newspapers across the country, and of course, no one at the White House, in Washington, or at the Air Transport Command in Memphis would take responsibility. "Somewhere down the line someone made a mistake," was as much as White House officials would admit. The press had a field day as editorials deplored the entire matter. Dog jokes were traded for days after in Congress, and even a senate subcommittee was convened to investigate the entire affair. On January 19, 1945, officials at the Air Transport Command, not surprisingly, announced that pets would no longer be provided transportation upon military aircraft. The incident loomed over Lt. Colonel Roosevelt like a dark cloud for the rest of the year, even as he was being considered for promotion to brigadier general.

Heights of 30 inches and weights of 130 pounds are common for the bull mastiff. It is an ancient breed, with records of the mastiff dating back to 3000 B.C. Egypt. The dogs have always been bred for their power and tenacity. Romans would match these huge dogs with bulls, bears, lions, and tigers, as well as humans in the Coliseum. They were introduced to Britain when the Romans invaded in 55 B.C., and were trained for dogfights in England when that "sport" was still legal.

Blaze himself was the apparent antithesis to Fala, Franklin Roosevelt's Scottie. To Fala's Jekyll, Blaze played Hyde. Fala was small and adorable; Blaze was large and rough. Fala accompanied Franklin D. Roosevelt almost everywhere, claiming a place of honor at Hyde Park; Blaze was sent to Hyde Park in 1945, after the Memphis incident, as a form of exile. Fala had been the centerpiece during one of Roosevelt's great political triumphs; Blaze was the cause of one of his more irritating embarrassments. And while many photographs of Fala can be found at the Franklin D. Roosevelt Library in Hyde Park today, not one picture of Blaze exists among the archives.

Finally, as a resident of Hyde Park, Blaze committed the most grievous of crimes. In the fall of 1945, Blaze, outweighing Fala by more than 100 pounds, attacked and badly mauled the little Scottie. But for the intercession of Eleanor Roosevelt's personal secretary, Malvina Thompson, Fala might have died. Instead, Thompson — or "Tommy," as she was called by Mrs. Roosevelt — pulled the Scottie away from Blaze, quite probably saving Fala's life. This was the Blaze's final transgression. Almost immediately, the ill-fated mastiff was ordered destroyed by the Roosevelt family.

SOURCES: American Kennel Club. *The Complete Dog Book*. New York: Howell, 1985. / Lash, Joseph P. *Eleanor: The Years Alone*. W.W. Norton, 1972. / *New York Times*, January 18–January 25, 1945.

Texas

ANIMAL: Old Rip
DOB: Unknown
DOD: January 29, 1929
DESCRIPTION: Horned toad (*Phrynosoma cornutum*), 5" long, grey scales.

The legend of Eastland, Texas, has nothing to do with cowboys. It's not about bandits or gunfighters or Indian warriors; it tells nothing of frontier woodsmen or Confederate soldiers or runaway slaves. It's about a horned toad.

The horned toad was named Ol' Rip, named after the character Rip Van Winkle in the classic tale by Washington Irving. In the story, Rip Van Winkle fell asleep under a shady tree in New England, and stayed asleep for 20 years. When he woke up, he found that the world around him had entirely changed. Like that of Rip Van Winkle, the legend of Ol' Rip contains a share of enchantment and intrigue.

On July 29, 1897, a small crowd gathered around the construction site for the new courthouse to be built in Eastland, 48 miles east of Abilene. Officials and citizens watched as justice of the peace Earnest Wood presided over the dedication of the foundation. Several items were placed inside the cornerstone — a Bible, photographs, newspaper clippings — in hopes that Eastlanders of the future could know something of their ancestors who erected the structure: Just before the ceremony ended and the cornerstone was sealed, young Will Wood, the son of the justice of the peace, also placed a horned toad into the cornerstone.

Actually, a horned toad is not a toad but a kind of lizard, related to the iguana. It is found in the dry plains of the Southwest, where it eats various insects and other small prey. Though rather ferocious and prehistoric-looking, with the ability to "spit" blood at would-be attackers, the horned toad is quite harmless, and even makes an excellent pet for a young boy. It is unclear why young Will Wood chose to place the reptile in the cornerstone. Since they are plentiful throughout Texas, and relatively easy to catch, perhaps Wood felt that this particular lizard would not be greatly missed. Like most young boys, Wood was no doubt curious, and perhaps simply wanted to see what would happen.

Thirty-one years later, on February 28, 1928, a larger crowd — between 1500 and 3000 people, depending on who tells the story — gathered around the courthouse site again. This time, the 1897 courthouse was being razed, to make way for a newer, larger courthouse.

Judge Edward Pritchard officiated at this ceremony, and Will Wood, now a man in his thirties, was again among the spectators. The cornerstone was opened, and the dingy, dusty, cold-blooded horned toad was removed from the

OLD RIP FACSIMILE
(courtesy of Eastland Chamber of Commerce)

slab. After several anxious moments, its tiny leg wiggled, and its eyes blinked open. It was alive! It had survived more than 11,132 days without food, water, air, or light! From that moment on, the horned lizard would be called "Ol' Rip."

Local biologists and naturalists, in discussing the veracity of Ol'Rip's story, do not dispute that the lizard could have hibernated through the winter months inside the cornerstone. The problem comes in accounting for the summer months. If the temperature inside the cornerstone ever became warm enough to arouse the lizard from his slumber, how would he have fed himself? Would cracks in the cornerstone have allowed ants or other insects into the concrete box, providing Ol' Rip with the nourishment he needed to survive through the years? If not, was it truly possible for one horned toad to survive in such a state for all those years? Or was the entire incident a hoax? Had the original lizard been replaced — perhaps several times — over the course of 31 years?

To the residents of Eastland, such questions were quite irrelevant. Once Ol' Rip emerged from his cell, he became an instant celebrity. Wire services carried the story around the nation and around the world. Ol' Rip became the subject of countless postcards, tie clips, T-shirts, and other tourist paraphernalia. An annual parade was established in his honor. The lizard and Will Wood, were even invited to the White House to visit with President Calvin "Silent Cal" Coolidge. Coolidge and Ol' Rip reportedly engaged in a staring contest during the visit, with inconclusive results. One story describes how, on the way home from Washington, Wood and Ol' Rip stopped off in St. Louis, where more than 40,000 curiosity seekers turned out to meet them.

The travel and pressure of fame apparently overwhelmed the horned lizard. He succumbed to pneumonia and died in January 1929. After surviving more than 30 years by himself in a granite box, life among the hordes killed him in less than 11 months.

Even in death, this unusual reptile couldn't escape controversy. It was decided that Ol' Rip's body would be embalmed and would lie in state in a transparent coffin in the Eastland County Courthouse. But even as Eastlanders filed respectfully past the reptile's remains, stories began to swirl again about the true identity of the carcass. Was this an imposter? Had Ol' Rip been toad-napped earlier, and replaced by some ordinary horned lizard to save Eastland County politicians from embarrassment?

So many mysteries for one horned lizard to carry to his death — yet there they lie, in the grave of Ol' Rip, as tourists from everywhere continue to pay their respects to the little glass coffin in the Eastland County Courthouse.

SOURCES: Lewis, Holden. "Horned Toad's Tale Dear to Hearts of Eastland Folks." *Abilene Reporter-News*, Sunday, December 17, 1989. P. 28A. / Macguire, Jack. "Eastland's Old Rip Packed Them In." *Abilene Reporter-News*, Sunday, July 30, 1989.

Utah

ANIMAL: Shasta
DOB: May 6, 1948
DOD: July 12, 1972
DESCRIPTION: Liger (*Panthera leo* and *Panthera tigris*), head like a tiger, body like a lioness, but lightly striped; 8' long, 375 pounds.

The birth of the most famous animal in the history of the state of Utah would not have been possible without zoos. For what happened at the Hogle Zoo in Salt Lake City could not have occurred in the wild.

In 1948, the native habitat of the lion was primarily the open plains of central and southeast Africa. A substantial population of lions had once existed in Asia, but by the mid–twentieth century it had all but vanished. The Bengal tiger's range is primarily the jungles of India. What's more, while the lion is a social animal, dwelling in prides of up to 20 adults, juveniles, and cubs, the tiger is a solitary hunter, seeking other tigers only when it is time to breed. Given the two animals' distribution and behavior, what happened in 1948 could only be engineered in a zoo.

Back in those days, zoos could often be likened to circus sideshows. The facilities and policies were designed primarily to entertain the visitors and reap profits for the zoo. The health, safety, and comfort of the animals were often secondary considerations. Thus, what happened in 1948 at the Hogle Zoo is very unlikely to happen today — even within the confines of a zoo.

The first United States–born liger to reach maturity arrived on May 6, 1948, at the Hogle Zoo in Salt Lake City, Utah. Other ligers had been born in zoos in Europe and Africa, but this animal outlived all the rest.

This liger was the offspring of male African lion named Huey and a female Bengal tiger named Daisy. Zoo officials had purposely housed the two felines in side-by-side cages in the Lion House. Huey and Daisy were encouraged to

SHASTA
(courtesy of Hogle Zoo, Salt Lake City)

become accustomed to each other, and later were attracted to each other. Finally they were brought together to mate.

At first Hogle Zoo officials claimed the cub was a tiglon. They were quickly corrected by *Time* magazine, however, which claimed there had been a tiglon-born of a male tiger and female lion — at Manhattan's Central Park Zoo.

Local lore holds that the liger cub was named "Shasta" by Mrs. Joseph Sloan. She and Mr. Sloan, who was then city parks superintendent for Salt Lake City, had taken the cub home to raise. Mrs. Sloan devised the name because she was always saying, "She hasta have her milk," or, "She hasta be let outside." Shasta was raised and bottle-fed like a domestic kitten until the age of three months. By then Shasta weighed 25 pounds, and the Sloan's household — particularly its breakable furniture — cried out for Shasta to be returned to the zoo.

Shasta's appearance and character were a true mixture of lion and tiger. She had a large lioness body, with a tiger-like head. Her body was a lionish tawny color, with light tiger stripes up and down her torso. She was reportedly less nervous than a tiger but more nervous than a lion, pacing up and down the cage in a tigerish manner. Full-grown, Shasta stretched to well over eight feet in length, and she weighed 375 pounds.

As the only mature liger in the United States, Shasta was quickly elevated to the status of local, national, and international celebrity. Each year, the zoo would celebrate Shasta's birthday with a birthday card party, sponsored by the *Salt Lake City Tribune*. Each child under 13 who brought a birthday card was admitted free. Over the years former kids brought their own kids, until generations had been delighted by the wondrous Shasta.

Of course, the media engulfed Shasta, who became the focus of endless articles and photo opportunties. Visitors from all around the world clamored to the view the curiosity. Extra attendance brought extra funds, which helped to finance the restoration of many of the zoo's once-dilapidated quarters. Shasta remained the center of attention for the Hogle Zoo from the first day of her life. She did not seem to mind the attention, however, and in fact seemed to take all the hoopla completely in stride.

Shasta spent the last weeks of her life in seclusion from the public, as her old and weary body rapidly failed. Though captive lions and tigers rarely live beyond their fifteenth year, Shasta lived to be 24. Finally, on July 12, 1972, Shasta died of kidney failure due to old age.

The oldest liger to live in the United States was stuffed, mounted, and initially displayed at the Museum of Natural History at the University of Utah. She was returned to Hogle Zoo in Salt Lake City in 1977 as a permanent fixture for the zoo. Though such works of taxidermy are not normally displayed in zoological gardens, the Hogle Zoo made an exception in Shasta's case, to ensure that "the children of today and tomorrow will believe what there parents and grandparents have told them."

SOURCES: *Desert News*, July 12, 1972. / Gudmundsen, Lance S. "Half Lion an' Tiger, Shasta the Liger Dies After 24 Years of Delighting Zoo Crowds." *Salt Lake City Tribune*, July 12, 1972.

Vermont

ANIMAL: Justin Morgan
DOB: 1789
DOD: 1821
DESCRIPTION: The Original Morgan Horse (*Equus caballus*), 14 hands high, 950 pounds.

Over the river and through the wood
To grandfather's house we go.
The horse knows the way to carry the sleigh
Through the white and drifted snow...

As the reader's mind conjures up images to go along with these words from Lydia Maria Child's poem "Thanksgiving Day," no doubt the horse conjured up is a Morgan. An ideal saddle horse, the Morgan is also strong in the harness, able to pull tremendous weights for its size. It is also capable of astonishing speed. The Morgan is the oldest of the American breeds, and is also the only breed of horse that developed from only one sire. And it is the only breed

THE MORGAN HORSE
(courtesy of the American Morgan Horse Association)

named after one specific horse, which has come to be known as the Justin Morgan horse.

The horse called Justin Morgan (whom historians believe was originally named Figure) was born in 1789 in Springfield, Massachusetts. His sire was True Briton, a Thoroughbred, and his unidentified dam is believed to have been of the Arabian breed. Named for his original owner, who was a school-master, Justin Morgan was taken to Randolph, Vermont, some 30 miles south of Montpelier. There, Justin Morgan's first owner died, and the horse changed owners several times. Over the next 32 years, he was recognized by those who worked him and rode him for his great strength as well as his swiftness as both a racer and a trotter.

Justin Morgan was relatively small (14 hands), but stocky (950 pounds), with a thick, muscular neck. Over the years he sired colts from a variety of mares, all of which retained traces of the sire: look, confirmation, longevity, stamina, and gentle deference. Over the years the colts grew to greater heights (by as much as six inches) and heavier weights (as much as 1200 pounds), but they kept the short legs, the deep chest, and the thick, rounded torso. The Morgan horse's popularity was especially high before the twentieth century, when Morgans were commonly found hitched to sleighs and carriages throughout the country, particularly around Vermont.

With the arrival of the horseless carriage, the Morgan struggled to find its niche. But as equestrians came to note the breed's versatility and endurance, the Morgan gained in popularity again, not only as a common farm and ranch horse, but as a show breed. The American Saddle Horse, the Standard-bred, and the Tennessee Walking Horse all trace their lineage to the Morgans. The original Justin Morgan horse died in 1821. A statue commemo-rating the first of the breed was erected at the University of Vermont in Wey-bridge. There, the university's agriculture department operates the Morgan Horse Farm, headquarters for the breed. University of Vermont students breed, raise, train, and show registered Morgans as part of their college curricu-lum.

The Justin Morgan horse was named Vermont's state animal in 1961.

SOURCES: Edwards, Margaret. *Justin Morgan: A Bicentennial Update.* American Mor-gan Horse Association, 1989. / Savitt, Sam. *America's Horses.* New York: Doubleday, 1966. / Walford, Bonny. *Champion Horses of the Americas.* New York: Galahad. Pp. 38–40.

Virginia

ANIMAL: Secretariat
DOB: March 30, 1970
DOD: October 4, 1989
DESCRIPTION: Thoroughbred horse (*Equus caballus*), chestnut coat, approximately 16 hands high.

There have been many great champions in horse racing, but the name "Superhorse" applies to only one. The only Triple Crown winner since Cita-tion in 1948, Secretariat won 16 of 21 races in his career, earning more than $1.3 million.

There was something regal about Secretariat, something almost charis-matic. The great chestnut always seemed to play to the crowd, and every race he ran in became something special. During his run to the Triple Crown, Sec-retariat captured and held the interest of media and the general public in a way that few horses ever do.

Secretariat was born March 30, 1970, at the Meadow in Doswell, Caro-line County, Virginia, sired by Bold Ruler. Owned by C.T. and Penny Tweedy Chenery, Secretariat raced under the Meadow's blue and white colors. He was trained by Lucien Lauren, and his jockey was Ron Turcotte.

In a career that spanned numerous special moments, Secretariat reached his pinnacle in 1973, when he won the three races that make up the Triple Crown — as follows:

SECRETARIAT
(courtesy of John Lee, New York Racing Association)

The Kentucky Derby, Churchill Downs, Louisville, Kentucky, April 28, 1973

Although the Kentucky Derby had been running continuously since 1874, it wasn't until 1902, under the promotion and management of Colonel Matt J. Winn, that it became an event of national interest. Today, this oldest continually run classic race is as much a part of the American sports scene as the World Series, the Superbowl, and the Indianapolis 500.

Although Secretariat was the favorite going into Churchill Downs, a race only a week before had proved he was not invincible. On April 21 a big, dark brown Thoroughbred named Sham had outdistanced Secretariat at the Wood Memorial at Aqueduct, New York. Sham would be Secretariat's greatest nemesis over the next six weeks.

Secretariat started the Derby in last place, trailing the field. The horse Shecky Green took the early lead, and Sham was also among the leaders.

At the first turn, Secretariat began to move up among the horses. By the eighth pole, Sham had taken the lead, but Secretariat was moving up beside him. The two horses were neck-and-neck for only a matter of moments; jockey Ron Turcotte tapped Secretariat's side three times, and "Superhorse" seemed to shift into some unknown gear, accelerating to a speed never seen in the last quarter-mile of the Derby. He blazed to the finish line, setting the mile and a quarter record of 1:59 ⅖, breaking the previous record set by Northern Dancer in 1964 by ⅗ of a second.

The Preakness, Pimlico Racetrack, Baltimore, Maryland, May 19, 1973

The Preakness is the second oldest of the Triple Crown races, established in 1873. The winner's trophy — called the Woodlawn Vase, created by Tiffany — was valued in 1983 at one million dollars. This is the richest trophy in North American sports. The big drawing card for the Preakness and Pimlico is that the residents of Baltimore and the mid–Atlantic seaboard all want to find out whether the winner of the Derby will go on undefeated to the third leg of the Triple Crown. Not unexpectedly, the city of Baltimore experienced its most horrendous traffic jam on May 19, 1973.

Sham was among the contenders for the mile and one-sixteenth at Pimlico, but the race was not nearly as close as the Derby. Starting in his customary trailing position, Secretariat swept around the entire field on the first turn. Laffit Pincay, the jockey for Sham, tried to counter Secretariat's move, but the big chestnut was simply too fast. Secretariat crossed the finish line two and one-half lengths ahead of Sham. His official time was 1:55, a full second less than the record set by Canonero II in 1971.

The Belmont Stakes, Belmont Park, New York, June 9, 1973

With the Triple Crown two-thirds claimed, Belmont Park was bedlam. Press corps from around the country and the world converged on New York. *Newsweek* and *Sports Illustrated* had given over their front covers to Secretariat, and it seemed as though Belmont Park was jammed with half the people in New York.

The Belmont Stakes had its one hundred and fifth running in 1973, making it the oldest of the Triple Crown races. The race had been run at Belmont Park since 1890, having been at Jerome Park from 1867 to 1888 and at Morris Park in 1889. At a mile and a half, it is the longest track in the Triple Crown.

In this race, Secretariat started out in the lead and held his position through the first straightaway. But at the turn, Pincay and Sham caught up, and going into the back stretch Sham took the lead. Sham's triumph was short-lived, to say the least. By the mile marker Secretariat was seven lengths ahead of Sham, and the remainder of the race was against no horse, but only the clock. Secretariat's time was 2:24, shattering Gallant Man's record by two and three-fifths seconds.

Secretariat was winner of the 1973 Triple Crown! Belmont Park went berserk!

"Superhorse" was retired to stud in 1973, after his final appearance on November 6 at Aqueduct. "Farewell to Secretariat" day drew more than 32,000 people, who cheered him as a hero. He retired at Clairborne Farms in Lexington, Kentucky, where he lived for the next 16 years.

In 1989, Secretariat developed an incurable hoof disease called laminitis, which causes inflammation and extreme pain in the hoof. The condition continued to worsen, until finally, to save him from suffering, Secretariat was destroyed on Wednesday, October 4, 1989.

"Superhorse" was gone. Surely, his like will never come again.

Thou shalt be the lord of all other animals.
Men shall follow thee wheresoever thou goest.
Good for pursuit as for flight, thou shalt fly
without wings.
Upon thy back shall riches repose,
and through thy means shall wealth come...
— Emir Ard-El-Kader,
Letter to General E. Daumas

SOURCES: Chew, Peter. *The Kentucky Derby: The First 100 Years.* Boston: Houghton Mifflin, 1974. / Woolfe, Raymond G., Jr. *Secretariat.* Radnor, Pa.: Chilton, 1974.

Washington

ANIMAL: Bozo
DOB: 1964
DESCRIPTION: Grizzly bear (*Ursus arctos*), approximately 7' tall, 375 to 450 pounds, cinnamon brown coat.

The power of television in today's society is truly remarkable. Instant celebrities can be made out of ordinary men and women, children, and even animals. In the 1970s, such celebrity descended on a bear named Bozo.

Bozo, a female grizzly bear, was born in 1964 and trained at the Olympic Game Farm in Sequim on the Olympic Peninsula, northwest across Puget Sound from Seattle and 75 miles north of Olympia, Washington. Bozo is now owned by Lloyd and Kathryn Beebe, who also own Olympic Game Farm, an animal park featuring beasts who have starred in television and movies.

In 1977, Sun Classic Pictures created a television movie, then a series, called "Life and Times of Grizzly Adams." Loosely based on the life of James "Grizzly" Adams, who was born in Massachusetts in 1812, the series was the story of a man who sought refuge in the Western wilderness after being accused of a crime he did not commit. The series presented a much more heroic character than the true Grizzly Adams, who, after abandoning his wife and kids, actually captured wild animals for zoos and circuses. In the series, Adams is portrayed as a gentle, nature-loving man, at peace with himself and the wilderness in which he lived. The series created the picture of an idyllic existence, much in contrast to the hustle and confusion of life in the late twentieth century.

Dan Hagerty was chosen to play the lead role in the series. The role of "Ben," Grizzly Adams' companion bear, went to Bozo. Her trainer, Terry Rowland, employed by Olympic Game Farm since 1965, was also hired by Sun Classic Pictures. For 16 weeks, the series episodes were filmed in the Uinta Mountains, Utah (or in Payson, Arizona, when the Utah weather turned sour). Each one hour episode took up to six days to film. The series premiered on NBC on September 28, 1977, with the final show airing on on July 26, 1978.

Haggerty had had some experience as an animal trainer in his youth and was therefore quite adept at playing the companion to a full-grown grizzly. Bozo was likewise the perfect choice for the series, thanks to her gentle personality, her unusual comfort level with people, and her trust in Rowland. Even during stunts — some requiring close contact with fire — Bozo readily cooperated. In turn, Rowland never hurt or threatened her; unlike other trainers in TV series involving semi-wild animals, Rowland never brought a firearm to the filming location. Rowland's philosophy was that if there was no gun available, everyone in the crew would have to be especially careful with the bear. They were, and there were no incidents during the filming.

While Rowlands' humane treatment of Bozo contributed greatly to the success of the filming, apparently the appeasement of Bozo's great appetite was equally important. Rowland used the grizzly's favorite food to inspire cooperation. One segment of filming required plying Bozo with 10 bags of marshmallows, two jars of jam, and several wieners. Bozo also appreciated helpings of red meat. At one point this menu created great concern for Bozo's weight, which blossomed to more than 450 pounds. But she eventually returned to a more respectable 375.

Although "The Life and Times of Grizzly Adams" ran for only a year, the series had an inestimable impact on the bear and the animal park. In 1977, the one year the series ran in prime time, Dan Haggerty visited Olympic Game Park Farm bringing the spotlight of celebrity and the media with him. That spotlight has remained with Bozo and the game park ever since. Today, more than 100,000 people come to visit the park each year. Without a doubt, say game park officials, the vast majority come to see Bozo, whom they recognize as "Ben" from "Grizzly Adams." Fans of the show come to Sequim just to see this bear, and to remember the series; to identify with her, and with the utopian lifestyle of their hero, Grizzly Adams.

SOURCES: Armstrong, Andre. "TV Star (man) Visits Sequim to Pose with Other Stars." *Port Angeles Daily News*, April 13, 1977. P. 1. / Mattila, Marlys. "Actress Bears Weight Well." *Port Angeles Daily News*, February 1, 1977. / Sweeney, Michael. "The Stars of the Game Farm: They're Bright…and Wild." *Seattle Post-Intelligencer*, November 30, 1980. P. A-1.

West Virginia

ANIMAL: Traveller
DOB: 1857
DOD: 1870
DESCRIPTION: Arabian Saddle horse (*Equus caballus*), iron-gray coat, 16 hands high.

TRAVELLER WITH GENERAL LEE
(courtesy of Virginia Historical Society, Richmond, Virginia)

Perhaps the most famous warhorse in American history was born in 1857 near Blue Sulphur Springs, Greenbrier County, in what is now West Virginia. The colt was raised by Captain James W. Johnson, who named it Jeff Davis. The colt took first premium at the Lewisburg fair in both 1859 and 1860, evidence of the integrity and nobility the steed would display continuously in later years.

In 1861, Captain Joseph M. Broun of the Wise Legion, the Army of Northern Virginia, bought the horse for $175 from Johnson when both men served together. Broun was immediately impressed with the strength, stamina, and temperament of Jeff Davis. He would say that Jeff Davis rarely needed urging, but eagerly strode forward at the slightest command, as if the horse could read the rider's mind.

General Robert E. Lee took command of the Wise Legion in the fall of 1861. Lee had seen Broun ride Jeff Davis on several occasions and was quite taken with the horse from the beginning. When the Third Regiment of the Army of West Virginia joined the Sixtieth Regiment of the Army of Virginia at Pocotaligo, South Carolina, Lee inquired to Broun about the colt. Broun offered the horse as a gift, to which the proud and ever-chivalrous Lee replied, "If you would willingly sell me the horse, I would gladly use it for a week or two to learn of its qualities." Broun was still reluctant to sell the horse to the general, wanting instead to give it to him outright.

Lee rode the horse for about a month and then returned it, saying he could not use it unless Broun sold it to him. Lee said he did not feel right using such a valuable horse unless it belonged to him. Broun finally consented, selling Jeff Davis to Lee in February 1862 for $200. It was the beginning of a relationship that would last beyond the completion of the Civil War. Almost immediately, Lee changed the name of the five-year-old to Traveller.

Traveller accompanied General Lee through some of the most famous events of the Civil War:

Battle of Antietam, Sharpsburg, Maryland , September 17, 1862

General Lee, in concert with General James Longstreet and General Stonewall Jackson, defeats Union general John Pope at Second Manassas on August 30. Lee then takes the offensive, advancing on General George McClellan's Army of the Potomac at Sharpsburg, Maryland, en route to Washington. On the bloodiest day of the war, McClellan meets the charging Lee, resulting in more than 10,000 casualties on both sides. Lee's invasion fails, but McClellan inexplicably decides not to pursue the retreating rebels.

Battle of Chancellorsville, Virginia, May 2–4, 1863

Lee takes on General Joseph Hooker, who replaced Ambrose Burnside, who replaced George McClellan as head of the Union army. Both sides lose another 10,000, but Lee also loses Stonewall Jackson, mistakenly shot behind the lines by one of his own men. The loss of Jackson may be the telling blow against the Confederates.

Gettysburg, Pennsylvania, July 1–3, 1863

In the three days of fierce fighting that are the turning point of the Civil War — and, perhaps, the course of American history — the Union army manages to hold its position on Culps Hill, Cemetery Ridge, and Big and Little Round Tops. Following the disaster of Pickett's Charge (General Lee's greatest military failure) the Confederate army limps dejectedly out of Pennsylvania, back to southern soil. In three days of battle, 28,000 Confederate soldiers were lost, to the Union's 23,000. But, of course, the Union could afford to lose much more. As his battered and weary soldiers stagger their way toward him, Lee sits bravely on Traveller, but his head is bowed. The general reassures his men, telling them they have all fought bravely and done as well as they possibly could; as to the matter of defeat, he says, "The fault is entirely mine."

Spotsylvania, Virginia, May 8–12, 1864

To the southeast of the Wilderness, 20,000 from both Confederate and Union troops are killed. The Battle of Spotsylvania features five days of almost continual fighting, often hand-to-hand.

Cold Harbor, Virginia, June 3, 1864

On the banks of the Chickahominy River, Lee's forces dig in an impreg-nable defense. In a military mistake that only later will Grant admit to, the Union commander ignores horrible losses of his own men to send wave after wave against the Army of Northern Virginia. General Lee, once more affixed upon his gray warhorse, urges his army on, which inflicts more than 60,000 casualties against Grant's continual war of attrition. Says one Southern general, "This is not war, it's murder!"

Appomattox Court House, Virginia, April 8, 1865

Surrounded by the Union army, his soldiers faced with starvation due to depletion of supplies, Robert E. Lee surrenders to General Grant. Given the use of Wilmer McLean's home at Appomattox Court House, the always proper and precise Lee rides out to meet his counterpart dressed in his best uniform, his side saber sparkling in the sun. Traveller's bridle and saddle are polished and gleaming, and horse and rider present the ultimate image of courage, dignity, and composure in the face of heartbreaking defeat.

At the end of the meeting, in which Grant offers generous terms to the surrendering Confederate troops, Grant and General Lee shake hands on the porch of McLean's house. Marching down the front steps, Lee climbs aboard Traveller and, wheeling the horse in the direction of the Union general, salutes while Traveller stands stock still.

In a heartrending scene, Lee returns from McLean's house to face his vanquished troops. Tattered and hungry soldiers crowd around their beloved commander to shake his hand, to touch his uniform, or to simply pass their hands across the coat of the noble Traveller. Even in defeat, Robert E. Lee rides with his head erect. Though his face is flushed, his eyes shining, and his heart crushing with sorrow, his countenance is clear, and his feelings are kept to himself. And, as usual, Traveller holds him upright, ever loyal and strong.

Lee and Traveller remained inseparable until death. At the funeral march of General Lee in 1870, Traveller was led by two soldiers behind the hearse carrying the general's remains, bridled and saddled with crepe. Traveller died a few months later, a victim of lockjaw. The horse's great skeleton stands now at the museum of Washington and Lee University. Of his great grey horse Lee once said:

> If I were an artist I would draw a picture of Traveller, representing his fine proportions, muscular figure, deep head, broad forehead, delicate ears, quick eye, small feet, black mane and tail. Such a picture would inspire a poet, whose genius could then depict his worth and describe his endurance of toil, hunger, thirst, heat and cold, and the dangers and sufferings through which he passed. He could dilate upon his sagacity and affection and his invariable response to every wish of his rider. He might imagine his thoughts through the long night marches and days of battle through which he passed. But I am no artist; I can only say he is a Confederate gray.

SOURCES: "General R.E. Lee's War Horse." *Richmond Dispatch*, August 10, 1886. / "Traveller Was a West Virginia Horse." *The Charleston Daily Mail*, December 27, 1925.

Wisconsin

ANIMAL: Old Abe
DOB: March 1861
DOD: March 28, 1881
DESCRIPTION: American bald eagle (*Haliaeetus leucocephalus*), deep brown wings and torso, snow white head, 40" long, 8' wingspan.

Ever since Congress selected the bald eagle as the national bird and emblem of the country in 1897, the American people have accorded this magnificent raptor a special status. It has been adored for its magnificent appearance, its regal stature, and its grandeur in flight. It has been revered for its steadfast loyalty, as male and female bald eagles mate for life. Yet, it has also been vilified as a coward, and a hunter of livestock and poultry. At one point it was also lamented, as DDT pesticide poisoning had brought the species to the edge of extinction.

Over the years, countless yarns have been spun concerning *Haliaeetus leucocephalus*, yarns containing both fact and fiction. Perhaps no story has been embellished with so much of both than the one concerning an American eagle, the state of Wisconsin, and the Civil War.

In the spring of 1861, near the mouth of the Jump River in what is now Chippewa County in northwest Wisconsin, a band of Flambeau Indians of the Chippewa Tribe invaded the nest of a mother eagle and captured a young eaglet from the nest. The tribe took the young raptor as its own, and brought it with them as they traded for goods with the Europeans who had settled along the Chippewa River, which branched off from the Jump. The wife of a farmer named Dan McCann traded some corn for the eagle, which became the family pet in the McCann home. It is said that while Dan McCann played the fiddle, the eagle would "dance" to the music, hopping about and flapping its wings to the tune.

At about the same time, a regiment of soldiers was being organized in the town of Eau Claire, at the southern end of the Chippewa River. This regiment was to become Wisconsin's contribution to the War Between the States, and the regiment was called Company C. McCann could not go off to war with his neighbors due to a leg injury, but, feeling compelled to do his part, he offered the eagle to the regiment as a mascot. The soldiers quickly named the eagle "Old Abe," and the regiment became known as the Eagle Regiment.

In a practice that would no doubt be condemned by the Audubon Society

OLD ABE
(courtesy of State Historical Society of Wisconsin)

today, a pole topped by a wooden perch was fashioned, and by means of a leather tie which allowed him to jump only a few inches above the perch, Old Abe was made to sit on the perch at the head of the regiment, to lead the Wisconsin Company into battle. Three tiny United States flags decorated the perch, emphasizing the importance of Old Abe's mascot role.

Old Abe appeared at 42 battles and skirmishes in which Company C engaged. Legend says the eagle would scream from his standard during battles, providing a morale boost for the soldiers. (Apparently, it never occurred to the company that the poor bird was probably terrified at the explosions and mayhem that surrounded it during the warfare.)

Confederates called Old Abe the "Yankee Buzzard," felt his presence was an aid to the Yankee cause, and tried to capture or destroy him several times, without success. Stories tell of Old Abe playing tricks on his soldier friends, stealing their food and knocking over their water buckets. The soldiers often shared their food with the eagle, and taught it to drink from a canteen.

One tale (however tall) tells of a soldier from Company C who was carrying Old Abe's perch at the Battle of Vicksburg. Rebel gunfire knocked the soldier off his feet, and he seemed doomed. But Old Abe spread his wings and flew skyward, dragging the standard and the soldier to safety.

Another time, Old Abe reportedly spotted a rebel soldier approaching the Union camp. Old Abe whistled to warn the company of the approaching enemy, and the Confederate was forthwith captured, thanks to Old Abe's eagle eye.

Finally, Old Abe's service to the Union army came to an end. On September 24, 1864, Captain Wolf of Company C presented Old Abe to the state of Wisconsin in a formal ceremony. Old Abe was kept in a cage in the capitol building basement for the rest of his life. He was brought out on special occasions, when dignitaries and onlookers would gawk and giggle at the old bird and his stories.

One February night in 1881, a fire started in the capitol basement. Old Abe suffered from smoke inhalation. From then on the eagle's health rapidly deteriorated, and he died on March 28, 1881. Old Abe's body was stuffed and mounted and placed on exhibition in Memorial Hall at the capitol. But the capitol was destroyed in a fire in 1904, along with Old Abe's age-worn body.

Replicas and paintings of Old Abe have since been commissioned to replace the original mounting. Old Abe and his tales are now enshrined forever in Memorial Hall and the Assembly Chamber of the Wisconsin Capitol.

SOURCES: *The Wisconsin Blue Book*. Wisconsin Legislative Reference Library, 1962. / Young, Patrick. *Old Abe: The Eagle Hero*. Englewood Cliffs, N.J.: Prentice Hall, 1965.

Wyoming

ANIMAL: Steamboat
DOB: 1898
DOD: 1914
DESCRIPTION: American Saddle Horse (*Equus caballus*), approximately 16 hands high, black coat, white "socks" on three of four feet.

Wyoming is and always will be the Cowboy State. The cowboy on his horse has come to symbolize the state of Wyoming. It is the emblem of the University of Wyoming. It appears in the House and Senate chambers in the state capitol. It even appears on the state license plates. And the horse upon which the cowboy rides is as much a part of the legend and symbol as the rider.

At the turn of the century, while the East and West coasts were embarked on the adventures of industrialization and modernization, Wyoming was still the wild range. Cowboys, ranches, rodeos, wild towns, and wild horses — all were, and still are, a vital part of the Wyoming economy, heritage, and heart.

STEAMBOAT
(courtesy of the Wyoming State Museum)

The wildest of all the wild horses was foaled at Frank Foss Ranch in Chugwater, Wyoming, about 33 miles north of Cheyenne. His father was a Percheron stallion, his mother a Mexican hot blood mare. He grew into a big, jet-black, powerful stallion with white "socks" on all but his left front hoof.

Frank Foss had sold the stallion to a ranchowner named Alexander Swan. In an age-old practice, cowboys castrated horses to reduce the amount of testosterone in their systems, making them easier to control. During the procedure, Swan's new horse bucked and hit his head so hard against the ground that he fractured a bone in his nose. The whistling sound emitted from his nose when he breathed inspired the name "Steamboat." The accident that gave him his name no doubt also contributed to his fiery disposition.

Steamboat was brought to the range of the Swan Land and Cattle Company, where cowboys tried to break his spirit and make him docile enough to work with. It never happened. A cowboy named Jimmy Danks, who apparently was the first to call him Steamboat, was the first to attempt to ride and control the stallion, to no avail. Rider after rider tried to rein him in, but most of them found themselves on their backsides, brushing the dust off their hats. Steamboat would not be tamed.

The powerful bucker's reputation spread throughout Wyoming, and he made his first rodeo appearance at the Festival of Mountain and Plain in Denver, Colorado, in 1901. Idaho cowboy Tom Minor, a rider of considerable experience and skill, was the first of many who tried, failed, and floundered in the dirt. For the next 12 years, Steamboat bucked and kicked and jumped, and hurled cowboys from his back. The few riders who managed to stay on him were treated to the horseride from hell. But, as legend has it, none of them ever controlled him, and Steamboat refused to be broken.

At the Albany County Fair in southeast Wyoming in 1903, University of Wyoming professor B.C. Buffum took a photograph of cowboy Guy Holt riding on the back of Steamboat. This picture is considered by many to be the classic image of bucking horse and rider, and it became the basis for the logo of the University of Wyoming in 1921.

In 1936, governor-to-be Lester Hunt commissioned Denver artist Allen True to create a design of a bucking bronco and rider for the Wyoming license plate. The logo True created is remarkably similar to the 1903 Buffum photograph, and though no one has proved it conclusively, many members of the Wyoming populace assume that the bronco gracing their license plates is the incomparable Steamboat.

In 1990, artist Peter M. Fillerup created a 14-foot sculpture of a cowboy riding a bucking bronco. The statue is now a permanent fixture at the University of Wyoming in Cody, 273 miles northwest of Casper. The caption at the bottom of the sculpture reads, "Fanning a Twister — Steamboat."

The image of the bucking bronco has endured as a popular image of the American West, not only in Wyoming, but throughout the United States. Unfortunately, the life of Steamboat did not last quite so long. The great Steamboat appeared in every major rodeo in and around Wyoming from 1901 to 1914. Then, in the fall of 1914, while appearing at a frontier show in Cheyenne, Steamboat was caught in a thunderstorm with several other horses. As the horses huddled together in a pen, the lightning spooked the herd. In the ensuing panic, Steamboat tripped and cut his leg on some barbed wire. He developed blood poisoning, and soon became deathly ill. In October of 1914, to end his terrible suffering, Steamboat was mercifully put to death.

SOURCES: Kane, Joseph Nathan. *Facts About the States.* New York: H.W. Wilson. P. 583. / Moulton, Candy Vyvey, and Moulton, Flossie. *Steamboat: Legendary Bucking Horse, His Life and Times.* Glendo, Wyo.: High Plains, 1992.

INDEX